# BRYAN ON IMPERIALISM

## William Jennings Bryan

ARNO PRESS & THE NEW YORK TIMES

New York ★ 1970

Collection Created and Selected
by
CHARLES GREGG OF GREGG PRESS


Reprinted from a copy in The New York Public Library

Library of Congress Catalog Card Number: 71-111701
ISBN 0-405-02005-8

ISBN for complete set: 0-405-02000-7




Reprint Edition 1970 by Arno Press Inc.
Manufactured in the United States of America

# BRYAN ON IMPERIALISM

Speeches, Newspaper Articles and Interviews

by

WILLIAM JENNINGS BRYAN

Chicago

BENTLEY & COMPANY

1900

[ *Title Page Reset for this Edition*
*Original Title Page Unavailable* ]

# FIRST SPEECH AGAINST IMPERIALISM.

"Nebraska is ready to do her part in time of war as well as in time of peace. Her citizens were among the first to give expression to their sympathy with the Cuban patriots, and her representatives in the Senate and House took a prominent part in the advocacy of armed intervention by the United States.

"When the President issued a call for volunteers Nebraska's quota was promptly furnished and she is prepared to respond to the second and subsequent calls.

"Nebraska's attitude upon the subject does not, however, indicate that the state is inhabited by a contentious or warlike people; it simply means that our people understand both the rights conferred, and the obligations imposed, by proximity to Cuba. Understanding these rights and obligations, they do not shrink from any consequences which may follow the performance of a national duty.

"War is harsh; it is attended by hardship and suffering; it means a vast expenditure of men and money. We may well pray for the coming of the day, promised in Holy Writ, when the swords shall be beaten into plowshares and the spears into pruning hooks; but universal peace cannot come until Justice is enthroned throughout the world. Jehovah deals with nations as He deals with men, and for both decrees that the wages of sin is death. Until the right has triumphed in every land and love reigns in every heart government must, as a last resort, appeal to force. As long as the oppressor is deaf to the voice of reason, so long must the citizen accustom his shoulder to the musket and his hand to the saber.

"Our nation exhausted diplomacy in its efforts to secure a peaceable solution of the Cuban question, and only took up arms when it was compelled to choose between war and servile acquiescence in cruelties which would have been a disgrace to barbarism.

"History will vindicate the position taken by the United States in the war with Spain. In saying this I assume that the principles which were invoked in the inauguration of the war

3

will be observed in its prosecution and conclusion. If, however, a contest undertaken for the sake of humanity degenerates into a war of conquest, we shall find it difficult to meet the charge of having added hypocrisy to greed. Is our national character so weak that we cannot withstand the temptation to appropriate the first piece of land that comes within our reach?

"To inflict upon the enemy all possible harm is legitimate warfare, but shall we contemplate a scheme for the colonization of the Orient merely because our ships won a remarkable victory in the harbor of Manila?

"Our guns destroyed a Spanish fleet, but can they destroy that self-evident truth, that governments derive their just powers, not from superior force, but from the consent of the governed?

"Shall we abandon a just resistance to European encroachment upon the Western hemisphere, in order to mingle in the controversies of Europe and Asia?

"Nebraska, standing midway between the oceans, will contribute her full share toward the protection of our sea coast; her sons will support the flag at home and abroad, wherever the honor and the interests of the nation may require. Nebraska will hold up the hands of the government while the battle rages, and when the war clouds roll away her voice will be heard pleading for the maintenance of those ideas which inspired the founders of our government and gave the nation its proud eminence among the nations of the earth.

"If others turn to thoughts of aggrandizement and yield allegiance to those who clothe land-covetousness in the attractive garb of 'national destiny' the people of Nebraska will, if I mistake not their sentiments, plant themselves upon the disclaimer entered by Congress and insist that good faith shall characterize the making of peace as it did the beginning of war. Goldsmith calls upon statesmen

"'* * * to judge how wide the limits stand
Betwixt a splendid and a happy land.'

"If some dream of the splendors of a heterogeneous empire encircling the globe, we shall be content to aid in bringing enduring happiness to a homogeneous people, consecrated to the purpose of maintaining a government of the people, by the people, and for the people."

[Extract from speech delivered at Trans-Mississippi Exposition, Omaha, Neb., June 14, 1898.]

# THE SAVANNAH INTERVIEW.

"My reason for leaving the army was set forth in my letter to the adjutant-general tendering my resignation. Now that the treaty of peace has been concluded I believe that I can be more useful to my country as a civilian than as a soldier.

"I may be in error, but in my judgment our nation is in greater danger just now than Cuba. Our people defended Cuba against foreign arms; now they must defend themselves and their country against a foreign idea—the colonial idea of European nations. Heretofore greed has perverted the government and used its instrumentalities for private gains, but now the very foundation principles of our government are assaulted. Our nation must give up any intention of entering upon a colonial policy, such as is now pursued by European countries, or it must abandon the doctrine that governments derive their just powers from the consent of the governed.

"To borrow a Bible quotation, 'A house divided against itself cannot stand.' Paraphrasing Lincoln's declaration, I may add that this nation cannot endure half republic and half colony—half free and half vassal. Our form of government, our traditions, our present interests and our future welfare, all forbid our entering upon a career of conquest.

"Jefferson has been quoted in support of imperialism, but our opponents must distinguish between imperialism and expansion; they must also distinguish between expansion in the western hemisphere and an expansion that involves us in the quarrels of Europe and the Orient. They must still further distinguish between expansion which secures contiguous territory for future settlement, and expansion which secures us alien races for future subjugation.

"Jefferson favored the annexation of necessary contiguous territory on the North American continent, but he was opposed to wars of conquest and expressly condemned the acquiring of remote territory.

"Some think that the fight should be made against ratification of the treaty, but I would prefer another plan. If the treaty is rejected, negotiations must be renewed and instead of settling the question according to our ideas we must settle it by diplomacy, with the possibility of international complications. It will be easier, I think, to end the war at once by ratifying the treaty and then deal with the subject in our own way. The issue can be presented directly by a resolution of Congress declaring the policy of the nation upon this subject. The President in his message says that our only purpose in taking possession of Cuba is to establish a stable government and then turn that government over to the people of Cuba. Congress could reaffirm this purpose in regard to Cuba and assert the same purpose in regard to the Philippines and Porto Rico. Such a resolution would make a clear-cut issue between the doctrine of self-government and the doctrine of imperialism. We should reserve a harbor and coaling station in Porto Rico and the Philippines in return for services rendered and I think we would be justified in asking the same concession from Cuba.

"In the case of Porto Rico, where the people have as yet expressed no desire for an independent government, we might with propriety declare our willingness to annex the island if the citizens desire annexation, but the Philippines are too far away and their people too different from ours to be annexed to the United States, even if they desired it."

[Interview at Savannah, Ga., December 13, 1898.]

---

## THE NATIONAL EMBLEM.

"The flag is a national emblem and is obedient to the national will. It was made for the people, not the people for the flag. When the American people want the flag raised, they raise it; when they want it hauled down, they haul it down. The flag was raised upon Canadian soil during the war of 1812 and it was hauled down when peace was restored. The flag was planted upon Chapultepec during the war with Mexico and it was hauled down when the war was over. The morning papers announce that General Lee ordered the flag hauled down in Cuba yesterday, because it was raised too soon. The flag will be raised in Cuba again on the 1st of January, but the President declares in his message that it will be hauled down as soon as a stable government is established. Who will deny to our people the right to haul the flag down in the Philippines, if they so desire, when a stable government is established there?

6

"Our flag stands for an indissoluble union of indestructible states. Every state is represented by a star and every territory sees in the constitution a star of hope that will some day take its place in the constellation. What is there in the flag to awaken the zeal or reflect the aspirations of vassal colonies which are too good to be cast away, but not good enough to be admitted to the sisterhood of states?

"Shall we keep the Philippines and amend our flag? Shall we add a new star—the blood-star, Mars—to indicate that we have entered upon a career of conquest? Or shall we borrow the yellow, which in 1896 was the badge of gold and greed, and paint Saturn and his rings, to suggest a carpet-bag government, with its schemes of spoliation? Or shall we adorn our flag with a milky way composed of a multitude of minor stars representing remote and insignificant dependencies?

"No, a thousand times better that we haul down the stars and stripes and substitute the flag of an independent republic than surrender the doctrines that give glory to 'Old Glory.' It was the flag of our fathers in the years that are gone; it is the flag of a reunited country to-day; let it be the flag of our nation in the years that are to come. Its stripes of red tell of the blood that was shed to purchase liberty; its stripes of white proclaim the pure and heaven-born purpose of a government which derives its just powers from the consent of the governed. The mission of that flag is to float—not over a conglomeration of commonwealths and colonies—but over 'the land of the free and the home of the brave;' and to that mission it must remain forever true—forever true."

[Extract from speech delivered at Lincoln, Neb., December 23, 1898, at reception tendered by The Woman's Bimetallic League, The Lancaster County Bimetallic League, and The University Bimetallic Club.]

---

## "WHO SAVES HIS COUNTRY SAVES HIMSELF."

"You have labored diligently to prevent foreign financiers from disregarding the rights of the American people; now you are called upon to use your influence to prevent the American people from disregarding the rights of others. Self-restraint is a difficult virtue to practice. Solomon says that 'he that ruleth his own spirit is better than he that taketh a city.' The American people have shown that they can take a city; will they be able to restrain the spirit of conquest?

7

"It has been the boast of our nation that right makes might; shall we abandon the motto of the republic and go back a century to the-monarchical motto which asserts that might makes right?

"Be not carried away by the excitement incident to war; it will soon subside. Our people will turn again to the paths of peace; justice will resume her reign.

"Be steadfast in the faith of the fathers; your fight is for yourselves as well as for your country. In the words of the distinguished Georgian Hill: 'Who saves his country saves himself—and all things saved do bless him. Who lets his country die, lets all things die, dies himself ignobly—and all things, dying, curse him.'

"Imperialism finds its inspiration in dollars, not in duty. It is not our duty to burden our people with increased taxes in order to give a few speculators an opportunity for exploitation; it is not our duty to sacrifice the best blood of our nation in tropical jungles in an attempt to stifle the very sentiments which have given vitality to American institutions; it is not our duty to deny to the people of the Philippines the rights for which our forefathers fought from Bunker Hill to Yorktown.

"Our nation has a mission, but it is to liberate those who are in bondage—not to place shackles upon those who are struggling to be free.

"We rejoice in the marvelous victory won by Dewey in Manila Bay; we would give to him a sacred place in history and crown his memory with blessings. To us he is a hero; to the Filipinos he can be a savior. Let him be known to posterity, not as the subjugator of an alien race, but as the redeemer of an oppressed people—not as a Lord Clive, but as a La Fayette. The gratitude of a people is better than a jeweled sword."

[Extract from speech delivered at Nebraska Traveling Men's Bryan Club banquet, Lincoln, Neb., December 31, 1898.]

## CINCINNATI SPEECH.

"The sentiment of the people upon any great question must be measured during the days of deliberation and not during the hours of excitement. A good man will sometimes be engaged in a fight, but it is not reasonable to expect a judicial

8

opinion from him until he has had time to wash the blood off his face.

"I have seen a herd of mild-eyed, gentle kine transferred into infuriated beasts by the sight and scent of blood, and I have seen the same animals quiet and peaceful again in a few hours.

"We have much of the animal in us still in spite of civilizing processes. It is not unnatural that our people should be more sanguinary immediately after a battle than they were before, but it is only a question of time when reflection will restore rne conditions which existed before this nation became engaged in the war with Spain.

"When men are excited they talk about what they can do; when they are calm they talk about what they ought to do.

"If the President rightly interpreted the feelings of the people when they were intoxicated by a military triumph we shall appeal from 'Philip drunk to Philip sober.' The forcible annexation of the Philippine Islands would violate a principle of American public law deeply imbedded in the American mind.

"It is difficult to overestimate the influence which such a change in our national policy would produce on the character of our people. Our opponents ask, is our nation not great enough to do what England, Germany and Holland are doing? They inquire, can we not govern colonies as well as they?

"Whether we can govern colonies as well as other countries can is not material; the real question is whether we can, in one hemisphere, develop the theory that governments derive their just power from the consent of the governed, and at the same time inaugurate, support and defend in the other hemisphere a government which derives its authority entirely from superior force.

"And if these two ideas of government cannot live together which one shall we choose? To defend forcible annexation on the ground that we are carrying out a religious duty is worse than absurd.

"The Bible teaches us that it is more blessed to give than to receive, while the colonial policy is based upon the doctrine that it is more blessed to take than to leave. I am afraid that the imperialists have confused the beatitudes.

9

"I once heard of a man who mixed up the parable of the good Samaritan with the parable of the sower, and in attempting to repeat the former, said:

"'A man went from Jerusalem to Jericho and as he went he fell among thorns and the thorns sprang up and choked him.'

"'We entered the Spanish war as peacemakers. Imperialists have an indistinct recollection that a blessing has been promised to the peacemakers and also to the meek, but their desire for more territory has perverted their memories, so that, as they recall the former, it reads: 'Blessed are the peacemakers, for they shall inherit the earth.'

"The meek are to inherit the earth, but the imperialists can hardly be classed among the meek.

"Annexation cannot be defended upon the ground that we shall find a pecuniary profit in the policy. The advantage which may come to a few individuals who hold the offices or who secure valuable franchises can not properly be weighed against the money expended in governing the Philippines, because the money expended will be paid by those who pay the taxes.

"We are not yet in position to determine whether the people of the United States as a whole will bring back from the Philippines as much as they send there. There is an old saying that it is not profitable to buy a lawsuit. Our nation may learn by experience that it is not wise to purchase the right to conquer a people.

"Spain, under compulsion, gives us a quit-claim to the Philippines in return for $20,000,000, but she does not agree to warrant and defend our title as against the Filipinos.

"To buy land is one thing; to buy people is another. Land is inanimate and makes no resistance to a transfer of title; the people are animate and sometimes desire a voice in their own affairs. But whether, measured by dollars and cents, the conquest of the Philippines would prove profitable or expensive, it will certainly prove embarrassing to those who still hold to the doctrine which underlies a republic.

"Military rule is antagonistic to our theory of government. The arguments which are used to defend it in the Philippines may be used to execute it in the United States.

10

"Under military rule much must be left to the discretion of the Military Governor, and this can only be justified upon the theory that the Governor knows more than the people whom he governs, is better acquainted with their needs than they are themselves, is entirely in sympathy with them, and is thoroughly honest and unselfish in his desire to do them good.

"Such a combination of wisdom, integrity and love is difficult to find and the Republican party will enter upon a hard task when it starts out to select suitable military Governors for our remote possessions.

"Even if the party has absolute confidence in its great political manager, Senator Hanna, it must be remembered that the people of Ohio have compelled him to serve them in the United States Senate, and that inferior men must be intrusted with the distribution of justice and benevolence among the nation's dark-skinned subjects in the Pacific.

"If we enter upon a colonial policy, we must expect to hear the command 'Silence' issuing with increasing emphasis from the imperialists. If a member of Congress attempts to criticise any injustice perpetrated by a government official against a helpless people he will be warned to keep silent lest his criticisms encourage resistance to American authority in the Orient.

"If an orator on the Fourth of July dares to speak of inalienable rights or refers with commendation to the manner in which our forefathers resisted taxation without representation he will be warned to kep silent lest his utterances excite rebellion among distant subjects.

"If we adopt a colonial policy and pursue the course which incited the revolution of 1776 we must muffle the tones of the old Liberty Bell and commune in whispers when we praise the patriotism of our forefathers.

"We cannot afford to destroy the Declaration of Independence; we cannot afford to erase from our constitutions, State and National, the bill of rights; we have not time to examine the libraries of the nation and purge them of the essays, the speeches, and the books that defend the doctrine that law is the crystallization of public opinion, rather than an emanation from physical power.

"But even if we could destroy every vestige of the laws which are the outgrowth of the immortal document penned by

11

Jefferson; if we could obliterate every written word that has been inspired by the idea that this is 'a government of the people, by the people, and for the people,' we could not tear from the heart of the human race the hope which the American republic has planted there. The impassioned appeal, 'Give me liberty or give me death,' still echoes around the world.

"In the future, as in the past, the desire to be free will be stronger than the desire to enjoy a mere physical existence. The conflict between right and might will continue here and everywhere until a day is reached when the love of money will no longer sear the national conscience and hypocrisy no longer hide the hideous features of avarice behind the mask of philanthropy."

[Extract from speech delivered at Duckworth Club banquet, Cincinnati, O., January 6, 1899.]

## JACKSON DAY SPEECH AT CHICAGO.

"Those who advocate the annexation of the Philippines call themselves expansionists, but they are really imperialists. The word expansion would describe the acquisition of territory to be populated by homogeneous people and to be carved into states like those now in existence. An empire suggests variety in race and diversity in government. The Imperialists do not desire to clothe the Filipinos with all the rights and privileges of American citizenship; they want to exercise sovereignty over an alien race and they expect to rule the new subjects upon a theory entirely at variance with constitutional government. Victoria is Queen of Great Britain and Empress of India; shall we change the title of our executive and call him the President of the United States and Emperor of the Philippines?

"The Democratic party stood for the money of the Constitution in 1896; it stands for the government of the Constitution now.

"It opposed an English financial policy in 1896; it opposes an English colonial policy now. Those who in 1896 were in favor of turning the American people over to the greed of foreign financiers and domestic trusts may now be willing to turn the Filipinos over to the tender mercies of military governors and carpet-bag officials.

12

"Those who in 1896 thought the people of the United States too weak to attend to their own business may now think them strong enough to attend to the business of remote and alien races; but those who, in 1896, fought for independence for the American people will not now withhold independence from those who desire it elsewhere.

"We are told that the Filipinos are not capable of self-government; that has a familiar ring. Only two years ago I heard the same argument made against a very respectable minority of the people of this country. The money loaners, who coerced borrowers, did it upon that theory; the employers who coerced their employes did it for the same reason. Self-government is a constant education; the capacity for self-government increases with participation in government. The Filipinos are not far enough advanced to share in the government of the people of the United States, but they are competent to govern themselves. It is not fair to compare them with our own citizens, because the American people have been educating themselves in the science of government for nearly three centuries and, while we have much to learn, we have already made great improvement. The Filipinos will not establish a perfect government, but they will establish a government as nearly perfect as they are competent to enjoy and the United States can protect them from molestation from without.

"Give the Filipinos time and opportunity, and while they never will catch up with us, unless we cease to improve, yet they may some day stand where we stand now.

"What excuse can be given for the adoption of a colonial policy? Secretary Gage disclosed the secret in his Savannah speech. I think we might be justified in calling Mr. Gage the key-hole of the administration, because we look through him to learn what is going on within the executive council chamber. He suggested that 'philanthropy and five per cent' would go hand in hand in the new venture. These are the two arguments which are always used in favor of conquest. 'Philanthropy and five per cent.' The one chloroforms the conscience of the conqueror and the other picks the pocket of the conquered.

"Some assert that we must hold the islands because of the pecuniary profit to be derived from them, while others say that

13

it is our duty to govern the Filipinos for their own good. I deny the soundness of both arguments. Forcible annexation will not only be 'criminal aggression' (to borrow Mr. McKinley's language of a year ago), but it will cost more than it is worth, and the whole people will pay the cost, while a few will reap all the benefits.

"Still weaker is the argument based upon religious duty. The Christian religion rests upon the doctrine of vicarious suffering; the colonial policy rests upon the doctrine of vicarious enjoyment.

"When the desire to steal becomes uncontrollable in an individual he is declared to be a kleptomaniac and is sent to an asylum; when the desire to grab land becomes uncontrollable in a nation we are told that the 'currents of destiny are flowing through the hearts of men' and that the American people are entering upon 'a manifest mission.'

"Shame upon a logic which locks up the petty offender and enthrones grand larceny. Have the people returned to the worship of the Golden Calf? Have they made unto themselves a new commandment consistent with the spirit of conquest and the lust for empire? Is 'thou shalt not steal upon a small scale' to be substituted for the law of Moses?

"Awake O ancient Law-Giver, awake! Break forth from thine unmarked sepulchre and speed thee back to cloud-crowned Sinai; commune once more with the God of our fathers and proclaim again the words engraven upon the tables of stone— the law that was, the law that is to-day—the law that neither individual nor nation can violate with impunity."

[Extract from speech delivered at banquet of Bryan League, Chicago, Ill., January 7, 1899.]

---

## NABOTH'S VINEYARD.

"The Bible tells us that Ahab, the king, wanted the vineyard of Naboth and was sorely grieved because the owner thereof refused to part with the inheritance of his fathers. Then followed a plot, and false charges were preferred against Naboth to furnish an excuse for getting rid of him.

"'Thou shalt not covet!' 'Thou shalt not bear false witness!' 'Thou shalt not kill'—three commandments broken, and still a fourth, 'Thou shalt not steal,' to be broken in order to get a little piece of ground! And what was the result? When the king went forth to take possession, Elijah, that brave old prophet of the early days, met him and pronounced against him the sentence of the Almighty: 'In the place where the dogs licked the blood of Naboth shall the dogs lick thy blood, even thine.'

"Neither his own exalted position nor the lowly station of his victim could save him from the avenging hand of outraged justice. His case was tried in a court where neither wealth, nor rank, nor power can shield the transgressor.

"Wars of conquest have their origin in covetousness, and the history of the human race has been written in characters of blood because rulers have looked with longing eyes upon the lands of others.

"Covetousness is prone to seek the aid of false pretence to carry out its plans, but what it cannot secure by persuasion it takes by the sword.

"Senator Teller's amendment to the intervention resolution saved the Cubans from the covetousness of those who are so anxious to secure possession of the island, that they are willing to deny the truth of the declaration of our own Congress, that 'the people of Cuba are, and of right ought to be free.'"

\* \* \*

"Imperialism might expand the nation's territory, but it would contract the nation's purpose. It is not a step forward toward a broader destiny; it is a step backward, toward the narrow views of kings and emperors.

"Dr. Taylor has aptly expressed it in his 'Creed of the Flag,' when he asks:

'Shall we turn to the old world again
With the penitent prodigal's cry?'

"I answer, never. This republic is not a prodigal son; it has not spent its substance in riotous living. It is not ready to retrace its steps and, with shamed face and trembling voice, solicit an humble place among the servants of royalty. It has ·not sinned against Heaven, and God grant that the crowned heads of Europe may never have occasion to kill the fatted calf to commemorate its return from reliance upon the will of the people to dependence upon the authority which flows from regal birth or superior force!

15

"We cannot afford to enter upon a colonial policy. The theory upon which a government is built is a matter of vital importance. The national idea has a controlling influence upon the thought and character of the people. Our national idea is self-government, and unless we are ready to abandon that idea forever we cannot ignore it in dealing with the Filipinos.

"That idea is entwined with our traditions; it permeates our history; it is a part of our literature.

"That idea has given eloquence to the orator and inspiration to the poet. Take from our national hymns the three words, free, freedom and liberty, and they would be as meaningless as would be our flag if robbed of its red, white and blue.

"Other nations may dream of wars of conquest and of distant dependencies governed by external force; not so with the United States.

"The fruits of imperialism, be they bitter or sweet, must be left to the subjects of monarchy. This is the one tree of which the citizens of a republic may not partake. It is the voice of the serpent, not the voice of God, that bids us eat."

[Extract from speech delivered in Denver. Colo., January 17, 1899, at the joint invitation of the Chairmen of the Democratic, Populist and Silver Republican State Committees.]

## LIBERTY, NOT CONQUEST.

The ratification of the treaty, instead of committing the United States to a colonial policy, really clears the way for the recognition of a Philippine republic. Lincoln, in his first inaugural message, condensed an unanswerable argument into a brief question when he asked, "Can aliens make treaties easier than friends can make laws?" The same argument is presented in the question, Could the independence of the Filipinos be secured more easily by diplomacy from a foreign and hostile nation than it can through laws passed by Congress and voicing the sentiments of the American people alone? If independence is more desirable to our people than a colonial policy who is there or what is there to prevent the recognition of Philippine independence? It is absurd to say that the United States can be transformed from a republic into an empire without consulting the voters.

16

The imperialists may be willing to deny to the Filipinos the right to govern themselves, but they cannot deny to the American people the right to determine the policy to be pursued by the United States in the settlement of the Philippine question.

Until the people express themselves we can only guess at their views, but is it not safer to suppose that they will adhere to the ideas and policies of a century than to assume that they will go back to the creed of kings and to the gospel of force?

In commemoration of the fact that France was our ally in securing independence the citizens of that nation joined with the citizens of the United States in placing in New York harbor an heroic statue representing Liberty enlightening the world. What course shall our nation pursue? Send the statue of Liberty back to France and borrow from England a statue of William the Conqueror? Or shall our nation so act as to enable the American people to join with the Filipinos in placing in the harbor of Manila a statue of Liberty enlightening the Orient?

[Extract from speech delivered at Democratic banquet, St Paul, Minn., February 14, 1899.]

## IT RESTS WITH THE PEOPLE.

The President, in his Boston speech, has declared that the future of the Philippines is in the hands of the American people. This is all that has been contended for by the opponents of the forcible and permanent annexation of the Philippine Islands. If the matter is in the hands of the American people, then it is a subject for discussion by the American people, and the only question to be considered and decided is whether the permanent retention of the Philippine Islands is desirable. In considering what is desirable we must consider what is best for the people of the United States, and what is best for the Filipinos. Those who oppose the colonial policy deny that the adoption of such a policy by this nation would be beneficial either to the United States or to the alien race over which our sovereignty would be extended.

The sooner the question is settled the better. It is putting the cart before the horse to say that the nation cannot reveal its purpose until the Filipinos lay down their arms. If the nation would declcare its intention to establish a stable and independent government in the Philippines and then leave that government in the hands of the people of the islands, hostilities would be suspended at once, and further bloodshed would be avoided.

What would our colonists have thought of a demand upon the part of England that we first lay down our arms and surrender to the king, and then trust to the decision that he would make? Now that the treaty has been ratified and Spain eliminated from the question, the American people are free to take such action as the circumstances require. Shall our nation enter upon a career of conquest and substitute the doctrine of force for the power of example and the influence of counsel?

Our forefathers fought for independence under a banner upon which was inscribed the motto, "Millions for defense, but not one cent for tribute." And so those who to-day not only desire American independence, but are willing to encourage the idea of independence and self-government in other races can fight under a banner upon which is inscribed a similar motto: "Millions for defense, but not one cent for conquest."'

Some of the advocates of a colonial policy have sought to lay upon those who opposed the ratification of the treaty the responsibility for the recent bloodshed at Manila. While I believed, and still believe, that it was better to ratify the treaty and make the fight for Philippine independence before the American people rather than through diplomatic negotiations with Spain, I deny that the Senators who opposed ratification were in any way responsible for the commencement of hostilities.

The responsibility rests, not upon those who opposed the treaty, but upon those who refused to disclose the nation's purpose, and left the Filipinos to believe that their fight against Spain, instead of bringing them independence, had only brought them a change of masters. It was the desire to be independent that led the Filipinos to resist American authority, and their desire for independence was not inspired by any American opposition to the terms of the treaty. It will be remembered that the Filipinos issued a declaration of independence last summer,

18

before the treaty was negotiated. Opposition to the treaty could not have caused a desire for independence which was expressed before the treaty was made. If it was wrong for any one in this country to inspire in other races a desire for self-government, the imperialists cannot confine their reproaches to the living. They must lay the blame upon American statesmen long since dead. Patrick Henry was responsible to some extent, because the sentiments he expressed in his speech have found a lodgment in the hearts of all races.

Washington must also be blamed, for when he drew his sword in defense of the rights of the colonists, he gave inspiration to all similarly situated. Jefferson was largely to blame, because the Declaration of Independence, the work of his pen, has been an inspiration to the lovers of liberty in every clime.

Abraham Lincoln cannot escape his share of blame if those are to be blamed who have aroused among the oppressed a desire for participation in the government under which they live. When the great emancipator delivered his speech at Gettysburg, and appealed to the people of the United States to so act that "a government of the people, for the people, and by the people shall not perish from the earth," he did more to stimulate the desire for self-government than has been done by any other public man in half a century.

The American people cannot apply the European and monarchical doctrine of force in the subjugation and government of alien races and at the same time stand forth as defenders of the principles embodied in our Declaration of Independence and Constitution. A man may live a double life when only one of his lives is known, but as soon as his duplicity becomes manifest to the world he can lead but one life, and that the worst. As soon as we establish two forms of government, one by consent in this country and the other by force in Asia, we shall cease to have the influence of a republic and shall join in the spoliation of helpless people under the pretense of conferring upon them unsought and undesired blessings.

Independence for the Filipinos under a protectorate which will guard them from outside interference while they work out their own destiny is consistent with American tradition, American history, and American interests. The sooner the declaration is made the better.

[Extract from speech delivered at State University, Ann Arbor, Mich., February 18, 1899.]
19

# AMERICA'S MISSION:

When the advocates of imperialism find it impossible to reconcile a colonial policy with the principles of our government or with the canons of morality; when they are unable to defend it upon the ground of religious duty or pecuniary profit, they fall back in helpless despair upon the assertion that it is destiny. "Suppose it does violate the constitution," they say; "suppose it does break all the commandments; suppose it does entail upon the nation an incalculable expenditure of blood and money; it is destiny and we must submit."

The people have not voted for imperialism; no national convention has declared for it; no Congress has passed upon it. To whom, then, has the future been revealed? Whence this voice of authority? We can all prophesy, but our prophesies are merely guesses, colored by our hopes and our surroundings. Man's opinion of what is to be is half wish and half environment. Avarice paints destiny with a dollar mark before it, militarism equips it with a sword.

He is the best prophet who, recognizing the omnipotence of truth, comprehends most clearly the great forces which are working out the progress, not of one party, not of one nation, but of the human race.

History is replete with predictions which once wore the hue of destiny, but which failed of fulfillment because those who uttered them saw too small an arc of the circle of events. When Pharaoh pursued the fleeing Israelites to the edge of the Red Sea he was confident that their bondage would be renewed and that they would again make bricks without straw, but destiny was not revealed until Moses and his followers reached the farther shore dry shod and the waves rolled over the horses and chariots of the Egyptians. When Belshazzar, on the last night of his reign, led his thousand lords into the Babylonian banquet hall and sat down to a table glittering with vessels of silver and gold he felt sure of his kingdom for many years to come, but destiny was not revealed until the hand wrote upon the wall those awe-inspiring words, "Mene, Mene, Tekel Upharsin." When Abderrahman swept northward with his conquering hosts his imagination saw the Crescent triumphant throughout the world, but destiny was not revealed until

20

Charles Martel raised the cross above the battlefield of Tours and saved Europe from the sword of Mohammedanism. When Napoleon emerged victorious from Marengo, from Ulm and from Austerlitz he thought himself the child of destiny, but destiny was not revealed until Blucher's forces joined the army of Wellington and the vanquished Corsican began his melancholy march toward St. Helena. When the redcoats of George the Third routed the New Englanders at Lexington and Bunker Hill there arose before the British sovereign visions of colonies taxed without representation and drained of their wealth by foreign-made laws, but destiny was not revealed until the surrender of Cornwallis completed the work begun at Independence Hall and ushered into existence a government deriving its just powers from the consent of the governed.

We have reached another crisis. The ancient doctrine of imperialism, banished from our land more than a century ago, has recrossed the Atlantic and challenged democracy to mortal combat upon American soil.

Whether the Spanish war shall be known in history as a war for liberty or as a war of conquest; whether the principles of self-government shall be strengthened or abandoned; whether this nation shall remain a homogeneous republic or become a heterogeneous empire—these questions must be answered by the American people—when they speak, and not until then, will destiny be revealed.

Destiny is not a matter of chance, it is a matter of choice; it is not a thing to be waited for, it is a thing to be achieved.

No one can see the end from the beginning, but every one can make his course an honorable one from beginning to end, by adhering to the right under all circumstances. Whether a man steals much or little may depend upon his opportunities, but whether he steals at all depends upon his own volition.

So with our nation. If we embark upon a career of conquest no one can tell how many islands we may be able to seize, or how many races we may be able to subjugate; neither can any one estimate the cost, immediate and remote, to the nation's purse and to the nation's character, but whether we shall enter upon such a career is a question which the people have a right to decide for themselves.

21

Unexpected events may retard or advance the nation's growth, but the nation's purpose determines its destiny.

What is the nation's purpose?

The main purpose of the founders of our government was to secure for themselves and for posterity the blessings of liberty, and that purpose has been faithfully followed up to this time. Our statesmen have opposed each other upon economic questions, but they have agreed in defending self-government as the controlling national idea. They have quarreled among themselves over tariff and finance, but they have been united in their opposition to an entangling alliance with any European power.

Under this policy our nation has grown in numbers and in strength. Under this policy its beneficent influence has encircled the globe. Under this policy the taxpayers have been spared the burden and the menace of a large military establishment and the young men have been taught the arts of peace rather than the science of war. On each returning Fourth of July our people have met to celebrate the signing of the Declaration of Independence; their hearts have renewed their vows to free institutions and their voices have praised the forefathers whose wisdom and courage and patriotism made it possible for each succeeding generation to repeat the words,

> "My country, 'tis of thee,
> Sweet land of liberty,
> Of thee I sing."

This sentiment was well-nigh universal until a year ago. It was to this sentiment that the Cuban insurgents appealed; it was this sentiment that impelled our people to enter into the war with Spain. Have the people so changed within a few short months that they are now willing to apologize for the War of the Revolution and force upon the Filipinos the same system of government against which the colonists protested with fire and sword?

The hour of temptation has come, but temptations do not destroy, they merely test the strength of individuals and nations; they are stumbling blocks or stepping-stones; they lead to infamy or fame, according to the use made of them.

Benedict Arnold and Ethan Allen served together in the Continental army and both were offered British gold. Arnold yielded to the temptation and made his name a synonym for treason; Allen resisted and lives in the affections of his countrymen.

Our nation is tempted to depart from its "standard of morality" and adopt a policy of "criminal aggression." But, will it yield?

If I mistake not the sentiment of the American people they will spurn the bribe of imperialism, and, by resisting temptation, win such a victory as has not been won since the battle of Yorktown. Let it be written of the United States: Behold a republic that took up arms to aid a neighboring people, struggling to be free; a republic that, in the progress of the war, helped distant races whose wrongs were not in contemplation when hostilities began; a republic that, when peace was restored, turned a deaf ear to the clamorous voice of greed and to those borne down by the weight of a foreign yoke, spoke the welcome words, Stand up; be free—let this be the record made on history's page and the silent example of this republic, true to its principles in the hour of trial, will do more to extend the area of self-government and civilization than could be done by all the wars of conquest that we could wage in a generation.

The forcible annexation of the Philippine Islands is not necessary to make the United States a world power. For over ten decades our nation has been a world power. During its brief existence it has exerted upon the human race an influence more potent for good than all the other nations of the earth combined, and it has exerted that influence without the use of sword or Gatling gun. Mexico and the republics of Central and South America testify to the benign influence of our institutions, while Europe and Asia give evidence of the working of the leaven of self-government. In the growth of democracy we observe the triumphant march of an idea—an idea that would be weighted down rather than aided by the armor and weapons proffered by imperialism.

Much has been said of late about Anglo-Saxon civilization. Far be it from me to detract from the service rendered to the world by the sturdy race whose language we speak. The union of the Angle and the Saxon formed a new and valuable type, but the process of race evolution was not completed when the Angle and the Saxon met. A still later type has appeared which

23

is superior to any which has existed heretofore; and with this new type will come a higher civilization than any which has preceded it. Great has been the Greek, the Latin, the Slav, the Celt, the Teuton and the Anglo-Saxon, but greater than any of these is the American, in whom are blended the virtues of them all.

Civil and religious liberty, universal education and the right to participate, directly or through representatives chosen by himself, in all the affairs of government—these give to the American citizen an opportunity and an inspiration which can be found nowhere else.

Standing upon the vantage ground already gained the American people can aspire to a grander destiny than has opened before any other race.

Anglo-Saxon civilization has taught the individual to protect his own rights, American civilization will teach him to respect the rights of others.

Anglo-Saxon civilization has taught the individual to take care of himself, American civilization, proclaiming the equality of all before the law, will teach him that his own highest good requires the observance of the commandment: "Thou shalt love thy neighbor as thyself."

Anglo-Saxon civilization has, by force of arms, applied the art of government to other races for the benefit of Anglo-Saxons; American civilization will, by the influence of example, excite in other races a desire for self-government and a determination to secure it.

Anglo-Saxon civilization has carried its flag to every clime and defended it with forts and garrisons. American civilization will imprint its flag upon the hearts of all who long for freedom.

To American civilization, all hail!

"Time's noblest offspring is the last!"

[Extract from speech delivered at Washington Day banquet given by the Virginia Democratic Association at Washington, D. C., February 22, 1899.]

# ARTICLES WRITTEN BY HON. W. J. BRYAN ON IMPERIALISM.

## JEFFERSON VERSUS IMPERIALISM.

The advocates of imperialism have sought to support their position by appealing to the authority of Jefferson. Of all the statesmen who have ever lived, Jefferson was the one most hostile to the doctrines embodied in the demand for a European colonial policy.

Imperialism as it now presents itself embraces four distinct propositions:

1. That the acquisition of territory by conquest is right.

2. That the acquisition of remote territory is desirable.

3. That the doctrine that governments derive their just powers from the consent of the governed is unsound.

4. That people can be wisely governed by aliens.

To all these propositions Jefferson was emphatically opposed. In a letter to William Short, written in 1791, he said:

"If there be one principle more deeply written than any other in the mind of every American, it is that we should have nothing to do with conquest."

Could he be more explicit? Here we have a clear and strong denunciation of the doctrine that territory should be acquired by force. If it is said that we have outgrown the ideas of the fathers, it may be observed that the doctrine laid down by Jefferson was reiterated only a few years ago by no less a Republican than James G. Blaine. All remember the enthusiasm with which he entered into the work of bringing the republics of North and South America into close and cordial relations; some, however, may have forgotten the resolutions introduced by him at the conference held in 1890, and approved by the commissioners present. They are as follows:

"First—That the principle of conquest, shall not, during the continuance of the treaty of arbitration, be recognized as admissible under American public law.

25

"Second—That all cessions of territory made during the continuance of the treaty of arbitration, shall be void if made under threats of war or in the presence of an armed force.

"Third—Any nation from which such cessions shall be exacted may demand that the validity of the cessions so made shall be submitted to arbitration.

"Fourth—Any renunciation of the right to arbitration made under the conditions named in the second section shall be null and void."

If the principle of conquest is right, why should it be denied a place in American public law? So objectionable is the theory of acquisition of territory by conquest that the nation which suffers such injustice can, according to the resolutions, recover by arbitration the land ceded in the presence of an armed force. So abhorrent is it, that a waiver of arbitration, made under such circumstances, is null and void. While the resolutions were only for the consideration of the American republics, the principle therein stated cannot be limited by latitude or longitude.

But this is a time of great and rapid changes, and some may even look upon Blaine's official acts as ancient history. If so, let it be remembered that President McKinley only a year ago (December 6, 1897), in a message to Congress discussing the Cuban situation, said:

"I speak not of forcible annexation, for that is not to be thought of. That, by our code of morality, would be criminal aggression."

And yet some are now thinking of that which was then "not to be thought of." Policy may change, but does a "code of morality" change? In his recent speech at Savannah, Secretary Gage, in defending the new policy of the administration, suggested that "philanthropy and five per cent" may go hand in hand. Surely we know not what a day may bring forth, if in so short a time "criminal aggression" can be transformed into "philanthropy and five per cent." What beauty, what riches, the isles of the Pacific must possess if they can tempt our people to abandon not only the traditions of a century, but our standard of national morality! What visions of national greatness the Philippines must arouse if the very sight of them can lead our country to vie with the monarchies of the old world in the extension of sovereignty by force.

26

Jefferson has been called an expansionist, but our opponents will search in vain for a single instance where he advocated the acquisition of remote territory. On the contrary, he expressly disclaimed any desire for land outside of the North American continent. That he looked forward to the annexation of Cuba is well known, but in a letter to President Monroe, dated June 23, 1823, he suggested that we should be in readiness to receive Cuba "when solicited by herself." To him Cuba was desirable only because of the island's close proximity to the United States. Thinking that some one might use the annexation of Cuba as a precedent for indefinite expansion, he said in a letter to President Madison, dated April 27, 1809:

"It will be objected to our receiving Cuba that no limit caʋ then be drawn to our future acquisitions," but, he added, "Cuba can be defended by us without a navy, and this develops the principle which ought to limit our views. Nothing should ever be accepted which would require a navy to defend it."

In the same letter, speaking of the possible acquisition of that island, he said:

"I would immediately erect a column on the southernmost limit of Cuba, and inscribe on it a ne plus ultra as to us in that direction."

It may be argued that Jefferson was wrong in asserting that we should confine our possessions to the North American continent, but certainly no one can truthfully quote him as an authority for excursions into the eastern hemisphere. If he was unwilling to go farther south than Cuba, even in the western hemisphere, would he be likely to look with favor upon colonies in the Orient?

If the authority of Jefferson cannot be invoked to support the acquisition of remote territory, much less can his great name be used to excuse a colonial policy which denies to the people the right to govern themselves. When he suggested an inscription for his monument he did not enumerate the honors which he had received, though no American had been more highly honored; he only asked to be remembered for what he had done, and he named the writing of the Declaration of Independence as the greatest of his deeds. In that memorable document he declared it a self-evident truth that governments derive their just powers from the consent of the governed. The defense and development of that doctrine was his special care. His writings abound with expressions showing his devotion to that doctrine and his solicitude for it. He preached it in the enthusiasm of his youth; he reiterated it when he reached the age of maturity; he crowned it with benedictions in his old age. Who will say that, if living, he would jeopardize it to-day by engrafting upon it the doctrine of government by external force?

Upon the fourth proposition Jefferson is no less explicit. Now, when some are suggesting the wisdom of a military government for the Philippines, or a colonial system such as England administers in India, it will not be out of place to refer to the manner in which Jefferson viewed the inability of aliens to prescribe laws and administer government. In 1817 a French society was formed for the purpose of settling upon a tract of land near the Tombigbee river. Jefferson was invited to formulate laws and regulations for the society. On the 16th of January of that year he wrote from Monticello expressing his high appreciation of the confidence expressed in him, but declining to undertake the task. The reasons he gave are well worth considering at this time. After wishing them great happiness in their undertaking he said:

"The laws, however, which must effect this must flow from their own habits, their own feelings, and the resources of their own minds. No stranger to these could possibly propose regulations adapted to them. Every people have their own particular habits, ways of thinking, manners, etc., which have grown up with them from their infancy, are become a part of their nature, and to which the regulations which are to make them happy must be accommodated. No member of a foreign country can have a sufficient sympathy with these. The institutions of Lycurgus, for example, would not have suited Athens, nor those of Solon, Lacedaemon. The organizations of Locke were impracticable for Carolina, and those of Rosseau for Poland. Turning inwardly on myself from these eminent illustrations of the truth of my observation, I feel all the presumption it would manifest should I undertake to do what this respectable society is alone qualified to do suitably for itself."

The alien may possess greater intelligence and greater strength, but he lacks the sympathy for, and the identification with, the people. We have only to recall the grievances enumerated in the Declaration of Independence to learn how an ocean may dilute justice and how the cry of the oppressed can be silenced by distance. And yet the inhabitants of the colonies were the descendants of Englishmen—blood of their blood and bone of their bone. Shall we be more considerate of subjects farther away from us, and differing from us in color, race and tongue, than the English were of their own offspring?

Modest Jefferson! He had been Governor, Ambassador to France, Vice-President and President; he was ripe in experience and crowned with honors; but this modern law-giver, this immortal genius, hesitated to suggest laws for a people with whose habits, customs and methods of thought he was unfamiliar. And yet the imperialists of to-day, intoxicated by a taste of blood, are rash enough to enter upon the government of the Filipinos, confident of the nation's ability to compel obedience, even if it cannot earn gratitude or win affection. Plutarch said that men entertained three sentiments concerning the ancient gods: They feared them for their strength, admired them for their wisdom and loved them for their justice. Jefferson taught the doctrine that governments should win the love of men. What shall be the ambition of our nation—to be loved because it is just or to be feared because it is strong.—Bryan in New York Journal, Dec. 25, 1898.

----

## THE ARMY.

In his annual message sent to Congress December 5, 1898, the President makes the following recommendations in favor of a permanent increase in the standing army:

"The importance of legislation for the permanent increase of the army is therefore manifest, and the recommendation of the Secretary of War for that purpose has my unqualified approval. There can be no question that at this time, and probably for some time in the future, one hundred thousand men will be none too many to meet the necessities of the situation."

It is strange that this request for so large an increase in the permanent army should be asked of a peace-loving people just at the time when the Czar of Russia is urging the nations of the world to join in the reduction of military establishments. But, strange as it may seem, the President not only requests it, but the Republican leaders in Congress seem inclined to grant the request.

Progress in Europe; retrogression in the United States!

In the old world "the currents of destiny" seem to be running in the direction of relief to the people from military burdens. Shall they run in an opposite direction here?

During the recent campaign the people were urged to support the party in power until the "fruits of victory" could be made secure. Is the first fruit of victory to be realized in the transfer of a large body of men from the field and workshop to the camp and barracks—from the ranks of the wealth producers to the ranks of the tax consumers? Such a transfer will lessen the nation's wealth-producing power and at the same time exact a larger annual tribute from those who toil.

Any unnecessary increase in the regular army is open to several objections, among which may be mentioned the following:

First—It increases taxes, and thus does injustice to those who contribute to the support of the Government.

Second—It tends to place force above reason in the structure of our Government.

Third—It lessens the nation's dependence upon its citizen soldiery—the sheet-anchor of a republic's defense.

No one objects to the maintenance of a regular army sufficient in strength to maintain law and order in time of peace and to form the nucleus of such an army as may be required when the military establishment is placed upon a war footing; but the taxpayers are justified in entering a vigorous protest against excessive appropriations for military purposes.

It is not surprising that the protest is most vigorous from the masses, because under our system of taxation the bulk of our Federal revenues is collected from import duties and internal revenue taxes upon liquors and tobaccos, all of which bear most heavily upon the poor. Import duties are collected upon articles used by the people, and the people do not use the articles taxed in proportion to income.

For instance, a man with an income of $100,000 does not eat, nor wear, nor use a hundred times as much of articles taxed as the average man with an income of $1,000. The people with small incomes, therefore, pay, as a rule, a larger percentage of their incomes to support the Federal Government than people with large incomes. The same is true of internal revenue taxes collected upon liquors and tobaccos. Men do not use liquor and tobacco in proportion to their incomes. Thus it will be seen that our Federal taxes are, in effect, an income tax; not only an income tax, but a graded income tax, and heaviest in proportion upon the smallest incomes.

If we could supply a part of our necessary revenues fr m a direct income tax the burdens of a large army would be more equitably borne, but, according to the decision of the Supreme Court, the income of an individual is more sacred than the individual, because the citizen can be drafted in time of danger, while his income cannot be taxed either in peace or war.

The army is the impersonation of force. It does not deliberate, it acts; it does not decide, it executes; it does not reason, it shoots.

Militarism is the very antithesis of Democracy; they do not grow in the same soil; they do not draw their nourishment from the same source.

In an army orders come down from the commander to the soldier, and the soldier obeys; in a republic mandates issue from the sovereign people, and the public servant gives heed. If any one doubts the demoralizing results which follow the use of force, even when that force is justified by necessity, let him behold the change which has taken place in the views of many of our people during the last eight months and then estimate, if he can, the far-reaching effect which a large increase in the permanent army would have upon the thoughts, the purposes and the character of our people.

Our Government derives its just powers from the consent of the governed, and its strength from the people themselves. We cannot afford to weaken the Government's reliance upon the people by cultivating the idea that all the work of war must be done by professional soldiers. The citizen is a safer lawmaker when he may be called upon to assist in the enforcement of the laws, and legislation is more likely to be just when the Government relies largely upon volunteers, because the support is surest when the Government is so beneficent that each citizen is willing to die to preserve its blessings to posterity. The readiness with which the American people have always responded to their country's call is a guarantee as to the future.

I have suggested some of the reasons (not all, by any means) why the regular army should not be increased, unless such increase be actually necessary. I now ask whether there is any such necessity for increasing that branch of the army which is held for service in the United States. There may, from time to time, be need of small additions to man new coast fortifications; but what is there in the domestic situation to justify or excuse the demand for more soldiers?

An army of occupation for service in Cuba, Porto Rico and the Philippines is made necessary by the conditions growing out of the war. But such an army is temporary in character, and should not be made a pretext for an increase of 200 per cent in our standing army.

The President assures us, in his last message, that the only purpose our Government has in taking possession of Cuba is to assist the Cubans in establishing a stable government. When that is accomplished our troops are to be withdrawn.

The number needed in the Philippines will depend largely upon the course pursued by the Government in regard to those islands. It will require fewer soldiers and less time to give self-government to the inhabitants of the Philippines than it will to give them a military government or a "carpet-bag" government. Since our standing army was sufficient for all domestic purposes prior to the war, and since there is much uncertainty in regard to the army of occupation, it would seem the part of wisdom to separate the two branches of the service and make provision at once for the latter, leaving the friends and opponents of a large standing army to settle that question after the volunteers are mustered out.

Most of the volunteers have no taste for military life; they left peaceful pursuits and enlisted, at a great sacrifice to themselves and their relatives, because their country needed them. Now that the war is over they desire to return home, and their desire should be gratified at the earliest possible moment. They were willing to fight when fighting was necessary; they were ready to lay down their arms as soon as hostilities ceased. If an attempt be made to secure a large increase in the army at home, merely because of a temporary need for an insular army, a prolonged Congressional debate is inevitable. Is it fair to keep the volunteers in the service while this question is being disposed of?

Unless Republican leaders desire to hold the volunteers as hostages to compel Congress to consent to a large army, they ought to be willing to postpone the consideration of the Regular Army bill and accept a substitute authorizing the President to recruit an army of occupation for service outside of the United States. The soldiers can be enlisted for two or three years, and before their term expires the nation's policy will be defined and conditions so settled that provision can be made for the future with more intelligence.

In recruiting the army of occupation opportunity should be given for the re-enlistment of such volunteers as desire to continue in the service. And I may add that it will encourage re-enlistment if a company or battalion formed from a volunteer regiment is allowed to select its officers from among the members of the regiment.

The pay of enlisted men serving in the army of occupation should be considerably increased over the present rate to compensate for greater risk to health incurred in the islands.

When the time arrives for the deliberate consideration of the permanent military establishment it will be found safer and more economical to provide complete modern equipment for the State militia, together with liberal appropriations for instruction and for annual encampments, than to increase the regular army. Soldiers in the regular service are withdrawn from productive labor and must be supported the year around, while members of the State militia receive military training without abandoning civil pursuits and without becoming a pecuniary burden to either State or Nation.

To recapitulate: There is no immediate necessity for the consideration of the proposition to permanently increase the military establishment; there is immediate necessity for the relief of the volunteers.

Let the army of occupation be recruited at once; let the size of the regular army be determined after the volunteers have been released.

The people are united in the desire to muster out the volunteers; they are divided in opinion in regard to the regular army.

Let each question be decided upon its merits.—New York Journal, Jan. 1, 1899.

33

# RATIFY THE TREATY, DECLARE THE NATION'S POLICY.

I gladly avail myself of the columns of the Journal to suggest a few reasons why the opponents of a colonial policy should make their fight in support of a resolution declaring the nation's purpose rather than against the ratification of the treaty.

The conflict between the doctrine of self-government and the doctrine of alien government supported by external force has been thrust upon the American people as a result of the war. It is so important a conflict that it cannot be avoided, and, since it deals with a question now before Congress, it must be considered immediately. It is useless to ask what effect this new issue will have upon other issues. Issues must be met as they arise; they cannot be moved about at will like pawns upon a chessboard.

The opponents of imperialism have an opportunity to choose the ground upon which the battle is to be fought. Why not oppose the ratification of the treaty?

First, because a victory won against the treaty would prove only temporary if the people really favor a colonial policy.

That a victory won against the treaty would depend for its value entirely upon the sentiment of the people is evident. A minority can obstruct action for a time, but a minority, so long as it remains a minority, can only delay action and enforce reflection; it cannot commit the nation to a policy.

When there seemed some probability of the rejection of the treaty the friends of the administration began to suggest the propriety of withholding the treaty until the new senate could be convened in extra session. As the new senate will have a considerable Republican majority it would be quite certain to ratify the treaty. Thus an effort to prevent the ratification of the treaty would be likely to fail in the very beginning. But let us suppose it possible to defeat ratification in both the present and the next senate—what would be the result? Would the imperialists abandon the hope of annexing the Philippines so long as they could claim the support of the President and a majority of both houses? Could a minority of the senate prevent the annexation of Hawaii? As we are now in possession of the Philippine Islands the advocates of a colonial policy might secure an appropriation sufficient to pay the twenty mil-

34

lions agreed upon and leave the rest of the treaty for future consideration. In other words, if the opponents of imperialism have a majority in both houses they can declare the nation's policy; if the imperialists have a majority in both houses they cannot be permanently thwarted by a minority in the Senate.

A resolution declaring the Nation's policy recognizes that the destiny of the United States is in the hands of all the people and seeks to ascertain at once the sentiment of the people as reflected by their representatives.

If that decision is in harmony with the policy which has prevailed in the past the question will be settled and the people will return to the consideration of domestic problems. If, however, the advocates of imperialism either postpone consideration or control the action of Congress an appeal will be taken to the voters at the next election. So great a change in our national policy cannot be made unless the authority therefor comes directly and unequivocally from that source of all power in a republic—the people.

In answer to those who fear that the question of imperialism, if discussed, will draw attention away from other questions, it is sufficient to say that the people cannot be prevented from considering a question which reaches down to the foundation principles of the republic. Instead of avoiding the issue it is the part of wisdom to deal with it at once and dispose of it permanently.

Second, the rejection of the treaty would be unwise because the opponents of the treaty would be compelled to assume responsibility for the continuance of war conditions and for the risks which always attend negotiations with a hostile nation.

The rejection of the treaty would give the administration an excuse for military expenditures which could not be justified after the conclusion of peace, and the opponents of the treaty would be charged with making such appropriations necessary. It must be remembered that in case the treaty is rejected negotiations must be renewed with an enemy whose ill-will is not concealed. Who is able to guarantee the Nation against new dangers and new complications? In order to form an estimate of the risks which would thus be incurred, one has only to recall the unexpected things which have happened since war was declared. Is it wise to so make the attack as to assume all the risks when the same end can be gained by a plan which throws the risks upon our opponents? If the imperialists vote down a resolution declaring the Nation's policy or postpone its consideration, they become responsible for any loss of life or expenditure of money which may follow as a result of such action.

I suggest below a few reasons in support of a resolution declaring it to be the Nation's purpose to establish a stable government in Cuba and the Philippines and then to give the inhabitants independence under an American protectorate which will guard them against molestation from without.

First, such a-course is consistent with national honor.

Our Nation owes it to the nations with which we have dealings, as well as to the inhabitants of Cuba, Porto Rico and the Philippines, to announce immediately what it intends to do respecting the territory surrendered by Spain.

The President has said that the only purpose our Nation has in taking possession of Cuba is to assist the inhabitants to establish a stable and independent government. It can do no harm for Congress to reaffirm this purpose, and it may do much good. The Cubans, having fought for independence for many years and against great odds, are naturally jealous of the liberty which they have won, and no doubt should be left as to the sincerity and good faith of our government in its dealings with them. Such a declaration would not only be harmless, but it is almost made necessary by the flippant, if not contemptuous, tone in which some United States officials speak of the intelligence and patriotism of the Cubans and of their right to independence.

The duty of declaring our national policy in regard to the Philippines is even more imperative. The Filipinos were fighting for independence when the United States declared war against Spain. In the formal protest filed with the peace commissioners in Paris the representatives of Aguinaldo assert that they received friendly assurances from United States officials and acted upon those assurances in co-operating against the Spaniards. Whether or not such assurances were given, frankness and honesty should characterize our dealings with them.

If we announce to the world that we hold the Philippine Islands, not for pecuniary profit but in trust for the inhabitants; if we declare that our only purpose is to assist the Filipinos to establish a stable and independent government, friendly relations will be maintained and there will be little need of troops. If, on the other hand, the Filipinos are not to have independence, but merely a change of masters, we should break the news to them at once and send over a large army to instruct them in the principles of a government which, in one hemisphere, derives its just powers from the consent of the governed, and in the other derives its authority from superior force.

While our Nation is not prepared to draft a complete code of laws suited to the peculiar needs of the Filipinos, we ought to be able to decide at once whether we intend to deal with them according to the principles of our own government or according to the customs prevailing among European monarchies. Even a Republican Congress ought to be able to choose without hesitation between a policy which establishes a republic in the Orient and a policy which sows the seeds of militarism in the United States.

The trade relations possible under a protectorate would be of more value to the United States than any which could come as the result of forcible annexation.

The people of Porto Rico have not manifested any desire for political independence, and would in all probability favor annexation, yet it is only right that they should have an opportunity to choose. The resolution authorizing intervention recognized the right of the Cubans to independence. To be consistent we must also respect the wishes of the inhabitants of Porto Rico. The resolution could, without impropriety, offer annexation to Porto Rico.

In a recent interview I suggested that the United States should retain a harbor and coaling station in the Philippines and in Porto Rico in return for services rendered, and added that Cuba should be asked to make a similar concession on the same ground.

Second, a resolution declaring the Nation's purpose presents a plain and clear-cut issue between the theory of self-government and the colonial policy. It presents a positive affirmative method of dealing with the question. In opposing the treaty we would be on the defensive; in outlining a policy we shall be aggressive. The strongest arguments which could be used in support of the treaty will lose their force entirely when Spain is eliminated and the American people are able to dispose of the question according to their own ideas and interests.

Third, it secures, by easier means, every end that can be secured by a rejection of the treaty.

If an officer of the law arrests a person in possession of stolen goods he can either compel the return of the goods to the owner or he can first rescue them and then return them himelf. We find Spain in the possession of a title to a part of the Philippines. She has not yet conquered all the native tribes, but the title which she has was acquired by force and has been held by force. We can either compel her to surrender her title to the Filipinos, as we compelled her to surrender Cuba to the Cubans, or we can accept possession and then of our own accord turn over the islands to the inhabitants. The peace commissioners might have demanded independence for the Filipinos as they did for the Cubans; if they did not properly interpret the wishes of the people of the United States the blame must fall upon them and not upon the people. Certainly seventy millions of citizens are under no obligation to abate their devotion to the ideals which they have cherished for a century in order to endorse the work of a peace commission or to approve of the instructions of an executive.

If it is urged that the ratification of the treaty imposes upon us an obligation to pay twenty millions of dollars to Spain, I answer, first, that this amount can probably be secured from the Filipinos in return for independence, and second, that, if it cannot be secured from them, it is better to lose the amount entirely than to expend a larger sum in securing a modification of the treaty.

It is better to regard the amount paid as a contribution to liberty than to consider it the market price of land, improvements. or people.

To terminate the war upon the same high plane upon which it was inaugurated is worthy of a great republic; to descend from a sublime beginning to the purchase of sovereignty (for our own profit) from a nation whose title we disputed in Cuba would lay us open to the charge of Punic faith.—New York Journal, Jan. 9, 1899.

# WILL IT PAY?

On former occasions I have quoted authority against the policy of imperialism and have insisted that the adoption of an European colonial policy would endanger the perpetuity of the republic. While every lover of his country should be willing to surrender a pecuniary advantage, however alluring, if that advantage would in the least jeopardize our national existence, still the opponents of imperialism are fortunate in having upon their side the dollar argument as well as the arguments based upon fundamental principles.

The forcible annexation of the Philippine Islands (and, in my judgment, even annexation by the consent of the people) would prove a source of pecuniary loss rather than gain. Heretofore our acquisitions have been confined to the North American continent, the Nation having in view either security from attack or land suitable for settlement. Generally both objects have been realized. Florida and the territory between the Mississippi and the Pacific were necessary for purposes of defense, and, in addition thereto, furnished homes and occupation for an increasing population.

The Hawaiian Islands are nearer to the western than to the eastern hemisphere, and their annexation was urged largely upon the ground that their possession by another nation would be a menace to the United States. When objection was made to the heterogeneous character of the people of the islands, it was met by the assertion that they were few in number. In the opinion of those who favored the annexation of Hawaii the advantages to be gained from a strategical standpoint outweighed the objection raised to the population. No argument made in favor of the annexation of the Hawaiian Islands can be used in support of the imperialistic policy. The purchase of Alaska removed one more monarchy from American territory and gave to the United States a maximum of land with a minimum of inhabitants.

In the forcible annexation of the Philippines our Nation neither adds to its strength nor secures broader opportunities for the American people.

Even if the principle of conquest were permissible under American public law, the conquest of territory so remote from our shores, inhabited by people who have no sympathy with our history or our customs, and who resent our attempt to over-throw their declaration of independence, would be a tax upon our military and naval strength the magnitude of which cannot now be determined.

Who can estimate in money and men the cost of subduing and keeping in subjection eight millions of people, six thousand miles away, scattered over twelve hundred islands and living under a tropical sun?

How many soldiers did Spain sacrifice in her effort to put down almost continuous insurrection in Cuba? How many perished from wounds and disease in the vain attempt to keep the Pearl of the Antilles under Spanish dominion? Yet Cuba has only about a million and a half of inhabitants, and Havana is only half as far from Cadiz as Manila is from San Francisco.

If this question is to be settled upon the basis of dollars and cents, who will insure the Nation that the receipts will equal the expenditures? Who will guarantee that the income from the Philippines, be it great or small, will find its way back to the pockets of the people who, through taxation, will furnish the money?

And even if the amount invested in ships, armament and in the equipment of soldiers is returned dollar for dollar, who will place a price upon the blood that will be shed? If war is to be waged for trade, how much trade ought to be demanded in exchange for a human life? And will the man who expects to secure the trade risk his own life or the life of some one else?

The demand for a standing army of one hundred thousand men is the beginning of a policy which will increase the hours of toil and fill the homes of the land with vacant chairs.

In his essay on the West Indies, Lord Macaulay denies that colonies are a source of profit even to European countries. He says:

"There are some who assert that, in a military and political point of view, the West Indies are of great importance to this country. This is a common but a monstrous misrepresentation. We venture to say that colonial empire has been one of the greatest curses of modern Europe. What nation has it ever strengthened? What nation has it ever enriched? What have been its fruits? Wars of frequent occurrence and immense cost, fettered trade, lavish expenditure, clashing jurisdiction, corruption in governments and indigence among the people. What have Mexico and Peru done for Spain, the Brazils for Portugal, Batavia for Holland? Or, if the experience of others is lost upon us, shall we not profit by our own? What have we not sacrificed to our infatuated passion for transatlantic dominion? This it is that has so often led us to risk our own smiling gardens and dear firesides for some snowy desert or infectious morass on the other side of the globe; this induced us to resign all the advantages of our insular situation—to embroil ourselves in the intrigues, and fight the battles of half the continent—to form coalitions which were instantly broken—and to give subsidies which were never earned; this gave birth to the fratricidal war against American liberty, with all its disgraceful defeats, and all its barren victories, and all the massacres of the Indian hatchet, and all the bloody contracts of the Hessian slaughter-house; this it was which, in the war against the French republic, induced us to send thousands and tens of thousands of our bravest troops to die in West Indian hospitals, while the armies of our enemies were pouring over the Rhine and the Alps. When a colonial acquisition has been in prospect, we have thought no expenditure extravagant, no interference perilous. Gold has been to us as dust, and blood as water. Shall we never learn wisdom? Shall we never cease to prosecute a pursuit wilder than the wildest dream of alchemy, with all the credulity and all the profusion of Sir Epicure Mammon?

"Those who maintain that settlements so remote conduce to the military or martime power of nations fly in the face of history."

Thus wrote England's orator, statesman and historian.

Shall we refuse to profit by the experience of others? Has the victory of seventy millions of people over seventeen millions so infatuated us with our own prowess that gold is to become to us also as dust and blood as water?

Let us consider for a moment the indirect cost of annexation. Grave domestic problems press for solution; can we afford to neglect them in order to engage unnecessarily in controversies abroad?

Must the people at large busy themselves with the contemplation of "destiny" while the special interests hedge themselves about with legal bulwarks and exact an increasing toll from productive industry?

41

While the American people are endeavoring to extend an unsolicited sovereignty over remote peoples, foreign financiers will be able to complete the conquest of our own country. Labor's protest against the black-list and government by injunction, and its plea for arbitration, shorter hours and a fair share of the wealth which it creates, will be drowned in noisy disputes over new boundary lines and in the clash of conflicting authority.

Monopoly can thrive in security so long as the inquiry, "Who will haul down the flag," on distant islands turns public attention away from the question, who will uproot the trusts at home?

What will it cost the people to substitute contests over treaties for economic issues? What will it cost the people to postpone consideration of remedial legislation while the ship of state tosses about in the whirlpool of international politics?

In considering the question of imperialism we have a right to weigh possibilities as well as certainties; and among the possibilities may be mentioned an offensive and defensive union between the United States and one or more European nations. Already one may hear an Anglo-American alliance suggested—a suggestion which would have been discarded as a dream a year ago. When this nation abandons its traditions and enters upon a colonial policy, a long step will have been taken toward those entanglements against which Washington and Jefferson with equal emphasis warned their countrymen.

What a 'change the imperialistic idea has already wrought in the minds of its advocates! During the Nation's infancy and development the American people spurned the thought of foreign alliance and its attendant obligations; they refused to yoke the young republic with a monarchy. The wisest among us are not able to measure the cost of a policy which would surrender the Nation's independence of action and drag it into the broils of Europe and Asia.

The Monroe doctrine, too, what will become of it? How can we expect European nations to respect our supremacy in the western hemisphere if we insist upon entering Asia? So long as we confine ourselves to our own continent we are strong enough to repel the world; but are we prepared (or is it worth while to prepare) to wage an offensive warfare in other parts of the globe?

On the other hand, what advantages are suggested by imperialists to offset the cost and dangers mentioned?

They tell us that trade follows the flag and that wider markets will be the result of annexation. Without admitting that any argument based upon trade advantages can justify an attempt to adopt a double standard in government—a government by consent in America and a government by force in Asia—it may be answered that commerce is a matter of cost and not a matter of bunting. The protectionist understands this and demands not a flag barrier but a price barrier between the home manufacturer and the foreign competitor.

Public attention has already been called to the fact that, while Spain was sending soldiers to the Philippines, England was sending merchandise. While the home government was sending money to the islands Great Britain was drawing money from them.

The cost of transportation is an important factor and has more influence than sovereignty in directing the course of trade.

Canada does not refuse to deal with us merely because she flies the British Jack; in fact, I have been told that she sometimes buys even her British Jacks in the United States. Our foreign trade is increasing, and that increase is not due to an expanding sovereignty.

The insignificance of the trade argument will be manifest to any one who will compare the consuming capacity of the Filipinos with that of a like number of Americans. The inhabitants of the torrid zones can never equal, or even approach, the inhabitants of the temperate zones as customers. England's commerce with the United States is greater than her commerce with India, and yet India has a population of nearly three hundred millions, and the English flag floats over them.

It is yet to be decided whether the open door policy will be adopted in the Orient or a tariff wall built around our subjects there, but neither plan will be found satisfactory. Our people, however, should not expect a colonial policy to prove acceptable, either to the governed or to the governing. If we attempt to run our country upon the European plan we must prepare ourselves for continual complaint. History has thus far failed to furnish a single example of a nation selfish enough to desire a colony and yet unselfish enough to govern it wisely at long range.

It has been argued that annexation would furnish a new field for the investment of American capital. If there is surplus money seeking investment, why is it not employed in the purchase of farm lands, in developing domestic enterprises or in replacing foreign capital? In 1896 we were told that we were dependent upon foreign capital and must so legislate as to keep what we had and invite more. Strange that it should be necessary to have an English financial system in order to bring European capital into the States and also an English colonial policy for the purpose of taking American capital out. Every dollar sent to the Philippines must be withdrawn from present investments, and we must either suffer to the extent of the amount withdrawn or borrow abroad and increase our bondage to foreign money-lenders.

It is sometimes suggested that the Philippines would furnish homes for those who are crowded out of this country. This argument, too, is without foundation. The population of the United States amounts to only twenty-one persons to the square mile, while the Philippine Islands already contain about sixty to the square mile. It will be several generations before the population of the United States will be as dense as it is now in the Philippines.

Our people will not flock to Manila; climatic conditions will be as great an obstacle as over-population. English supremacy in India has continued for nearly a hundred and fifty years, and yet in 1891 the British-born population of India was only 100,551 —less than the total number of prisoners confined in the jails of India at the end of 1895.

Jamaica has had all the advantages which could be derived from an English colonial policy, and yet the white population in 1891 numbered less than fifteen thousand out of a total of 639,000.

Java has been under the dominion of the Netherlands for nearly three hundred years, and yet in 1894 the Europeans upon the island numbered less than 60,000 out of a total population of more than 25,000,000.

Spain has been able to induce but a small number of her people to settle in the Philippines, and, if we can judge from the reports sent back by our volunteers, we shall not succeed any better.

But while the Philippines will not prove inviting to Americans, we shall probably draw a considerable number from the islands to the United States. The emigration will be eastward rather. than westward. During the six years from 1889 to 1894 more than ninety thousand coolies left India, and we may expect an influx of Malays.

It is not strange that the laboring men should look with undisguised alarm upon the prospect of oriental competition upon the farms and in the factories of the United States. Our people have legislated against Chinese emigration, but to exclude a few Chinese and admit many Filipinos is like straining at a gnat and swallowing a camel.

The farmers and laboring men constitute a large majority of the American people; what is there in annexation for them? Heavier taxes, Asiatic emigration and an opportunity to furnish more sons for the army.

Will it pay?—New York Journal, Jan. 15, 1899.

---

## BRITISH RULE IN INDIA.

In the discussion of a colonial policy for the United States frequent references will be made to England's government of India. The imperialists are already declaring that Great Britain's policy has resulted in profit to herself and benefit to her Asiatic subjects.

The opponents of imperialism, on the other hand, find in India's experience a warning against a policy which places one nation under the control of another and distant nation.

In 1600 the first East India company was organized. Its charter was for fifteen years, but a new and perpetual charter was granted in 1609. Under the reign of Charles II. the company obtained another charter which continued former privileges and added authority "to make peace or war with any prince or people (in India) not being Christian."

The affairs of the company were managed with an eye single to gain, and intervention in the quarrels of native princes resulted in the gradual extension of its influence. Money was the object, and the means employed would not always bear scrutiny. There was, however, no hypocritical mingling of an imaginary "philanthropy" with an actual "five per cent."

45

In 1757 Lord Clive, by the battle of Plassey, made the company the dominant power in Indian politics, and under Clive and Hastings the income of the East India Company reached enormous proportions.

The history of the century, beginning with the battle of Plassey and ending with the Sepoy mutiny in 1857, was written under headlines like the following: "The First War with Hyder Ali," "The Rohilla War," "The Second War with Hyder Ali," "The War with Tippoo Saib," "The War with the Mahrattas," "Suppression of the Pindaris," "The Last of the Peshwas," "The First Burmese War," "The First Afghan War," "The Conquest of Scinde," "The Sekh Wars," "The Conquest of Punjab," "The Annexation of Pegu," "The Annexation of Oudh," "The Outbreak of Meerut," "The Seizure of Delhi," "The Siege of Lucknow," etc., etc.

This brief review is not given because it is interesting, but to acquaint the reader with the imperialistic plan of solving the problem of civilization by the elimination of unruly factors.

In 1858 Parliament, by an act entitled an act "for the better government of India," confessed that the management of Indian affairs could be improved and placed the control in the hands of a Secretary of State for India and a Council.

In 1877 Queen Victoria assumed the title, Empress of India.

Even if it could be shown that England's sovereignty over India had brought blessings to the Indian people and advantage to the inhabitants of Great Britain, we could not afford to adopt the policy. A monarchy can engage in work which a republic dare not undertake. A monarchy is constructed upon the theory that authority descends from the king and that privileges are granted by the crown to the subjects. Of course the ruling power recognizes that it owes a duty to the people, but while the obligation is binding upon the conscience of the sovereign it cannot be enforced by the subject.

Webster presented this idea with great force in his speech on the Greek revolution. After setting forth the agreement between the Allied Powers, he said: "The first of these principles is, that all popular or constitutional rights are holden no otherwise than as grants from the crown. Society, upon this principle, has no rights of its own; it takes good government, when it gets it, as a boon and a concession, but can demand nothing. It is to live in that favor which emanates from royal authority, and if it have the misfortune to lose that favor, there is nothing to protect it against any degree of injustice and oppression. It can rightfully make no endeavor for a change, by itself; its whole privilege is to receive the favors that may be dispensed by the sovereign power, and all its duty is described in the single word, submission. This is the plain result of the principal continental state papers; indeed, it is nearly the identical text of some of them."

The English people have from time to time forced the crown to recognize certain rights, but the principle of monarchy still exists. The sovereign has a veto upon all legislation; the fact that this veto has not been used of late does not change the governmental theory, and, in India, the application of the theory has deprived the Indian people of participation in the control of their own affairs.

A nation which denies the principle that governments derive their just powers from the consent of the governed can give self-government to one colony and deny it to another; it can give it to colonies strong enough to exact it by force and deny it to weaker ones; but a nation which recognizes the people as the only sovereigns, and regards those temporarily in authority merely as public servants, is not at liberty to apply the principle to one section of the country and refuse it to another.

But, so far from supporting the contention of the imperialists, British rule in India really enforces every argument that can be made against a colonial system of government. In the first place, to authorize a commercial company "to make peace or war with any prince or people (not Christian)," according to its pleasure, was to place the pecuniary interests of a few stockholders above the rights of those with whom they had dealings. Clive and Hastings seem to have acted upon this authority. When the former was called to account he confessed that he had forged a treaty, and his conduct was such that Parliament was compelled to vote that he "had abused his powers and set an evil example to the servants of the public," but, as he had increased the power of England in India, his condemnation was accompanied by the declaration that he had, "at the same time, rendered great and meritorious services to his country."

47

The prosecution of Hastings for wrongs inflicted upon the people of India occupies a conspicuous place among the political trials of history. The speeches made against him recall the orations of Cicero against Verres, who, by the way, was also charged with plundering a colony.

Cicero said that Verres relied for his hope of escape upon his ability to corrupt the judges of his day, and it appears that the East India Company was also accused of polluting the stream of justice only a century ago.

In his speech on the Nabob of Arcot's debts, Burke said: "Let no man hereafter talk of the decaying energies of nature. All the acts and monuments in the records of peculation; the consolidated corruption of ages; the pattern of exemplary plunder in the heroic times of Roman iniquity, never equaled the gigantic corruption of this single act. Never did Nero, in all his insolent prodigality of despotism, deal out to his praetorian guards a donation fit to be named with the largess showered down by the bounty of our chancellor of the exchequer on the faithful band of Indian sepoys."

How little human nature changes from age to age! How weak is the boasted strength of the arm of the law when the defendant possesses the influence purchased by great wealth, however obtained, and the accusation comes from a far-off victim of oppression!

Those who expect justice to be exercised by officials far removed from the source of power—officials who do not receive their commissions from, and cannot be removed by, the people whom they govern—should read Sheridan's great speech portraying the effect of the Hastings policy upon the people of India.

Below will be found an extract:

"If, my lords, a stranger had at this time entered the province of Oude, ignorant of what had happened since the death of Sujah Dowlah, that prince who, with a savage heart, had still great lines of character, and who, with all his ferocity in war, had with a cultivating hand preserved to his country the wealth which it derived from benignant skies, and a prolific soil; if observing the wide and general devastation of fields unclothed and brown; of vegetation burnt up and extinguished; of villages depopulated and in ruin; of temples unroofed and perishing; of reservoirs broken down and dry, this stranger would ask, 'What has thus laid waste this beautiful and opulent land; what monstrous madness has ravaged with widespread war; what desolating foreign foe; what civil discords; what disputed succession; what religious zeal; what fabled monster has stalked abroad, and, with malice and mortal enmity to man, withered by the grasp of death every growth of nature and humanity, all means of delight, and each original, simple principle of bare existence? The answer would have been: Not one of these causes! No wars have ravaged these lands and depopulated these villages! No desolating foreign foe, no domestic broils, no disputed succession, no religious superserviceable zeal, no poisonous monster, no affliction of Providence, which, while it scourges us, cut off the sources of resuscitation!

"No. This damp of death is the mere effusion of British amity! We sink under the pressure of their support! We writhe under their perfidious gripe! They have embraced us with their protecting arms, and lo! these are the fruits of their alliance!"

No clearer case was ever made against a prisoner at the bar, and yet after a seven years' trial before the House of Lords Hastings was acquitted, not because he was guiltless, but because England had acquired territory by his policy.

Lord Macaulay, in describing the crimes perpetrated at that time against a helpless people, gives expression to a truth which has lost none of its force with the lapse of years. He says: "And then was seen what we believe to be the most frightful of all spectacles, the strength of civilization without its mercy. To all other despotism there is a check, imperfect indeed, and liable to gross abuse, but still sufficient to preserve society from the last extreme of misery. A time comes when the evils of submission are obviously greater than those of resistance, when fear itself begets a sort of courage, when a convulsive burst of popular rage and despair warns tyrants not to presume too far on the patience of mankind. But against misgovernment such as then afflicted Bengal, it is impossible to struggle. The superior intelligence and energy of the dominant class made their power irresistible. A war of Bengalees against Englishmen was like a war of sheep against wolves, of men against demons."

"The strength of civilization without its mercy!"

The American people are capable of governing themselves, but what reason have we to believe that they can wisely administer the affairs of distant races? It is difficult enough to curb corporate power in this country, where the people who suffer have in their own hands the means of redress; how much more difficult it would be to protect the interests of the people where the people who do the governing do not feel the suffering and where the people who do the suffering must rely upon the mercy of alien rulers!

True, Macaulay argues that English morality, tardily but finally, followed English authority into the Orient, but, as a matter of fact, the bleeding of India has continued systematically during the present century. Polite and refined methods have been substituted for the rude and harsh ones formerly employed, and the money received is distributed among a larger number, but the total sum annually drawn from India is greater now than it was when England's foremost orators and statesmen were demanding the impeachment of notorious malefactors.

Sir J. Strachey, an Englishman, in a history recently published, is quoted as saying that "the confiscation of the rights of the ryots (in Bengal) has reached vast proportions." He then shows that through the action of the English government the Zemindars, or middle men, have been able to enormously increase their income at the expense of the tillers of the soil, the increase being from four hundred thousand pounds in the last century to thirteen million pounds at the present time.

On the 28th of December, 1897—only a year ago—a meeting of the London Indian Society was held at Montague Mansions and strong resolutions adopted. Below will be found an extract from the resolutions:

"That this conference of Indians, resident in the United Kingdom, is of opinion—

"That of all the evils and 'terrible misery' that India has been suffering for a century and a half, and of which the latest developments are the most deplorable, famine and plague, arising from ever-increasing poverty, the stupid and suicidal Frontier War and its savagery, of the wholsale destruction of villages, unworthy of any people, but far more so of English civilization; the unwise and suicidal prosecutions for sedition; the absurd and ignorant cry of the disloyalty of the educated Indians, and for the curtailment of the liberty of the Indian press; the despotism—like that of the imprisonment of the Natus, and the general insufficiency and inefficiency of the administration —of all these and many other minor evils the main cause is the unrighteous and un-British system of government which produces an unceasing and ever-increasing bleeding of the country, and which is maintained by a political hypocrisy and continuous subterfuges unworthy of the British honor and name, and entirely in opposition to the wishes of the British people, and utterly in violation of acts and resolutions of Parliament, and of the most solemn and repeated pledges of the British nation and sovereign.

"That unless the present unrighteous and un-British system of government is thoroughly reformed into a righteous and truly British system destruction to India and disaster to the British empire must be the inevitable result."

Mr. Naoroji, an Indian residing in England, in supporting the resolution, pointed out the continuous drain of money from India and argued that the people were compelled "to make brick, not only without straw, but even without clay." He insisted that England's trade with India would be greater if she would allow the people of India a larger participation in the affairs of their own government, and protested against the policy of send ing Englishmen to India to hold the offices and draw their support from taxes levied upon the inhabitants. He complained that British justice is one thing in England and quite another thing in India, and said: "There (in India) it is only the business of the people to pay taxes and to slave; and the business of the government to spend those taxes to their own benefit. Whenever any question arises between Great Britain and India there is a demoralized mind. The principles of politics, of commerce, of equality which are applied to Great Britain are not applied to India. As if it were not inhabited by human beings!"

Does any one doubt that, if we annex the Philippines and govern them by agents sent from here, questions between them and the people of the United States will be settled by the people of the United States and for the benefit of the people of the United .States? If we make subjects of them against their will and for our own benefit are we likely to govern them with any more benevolence?

The resolutions quoted mention efforts for the curtailment of the liberty of the press. Is that not a necessary result of governmental injustice? Are we likely to allow the Filipinos freedom of the press, if we enter upon a system that is indefensible according to our theory of government?

Mr. Hyndman, an English writer, in a pamphlet issued in 1897, calls attention to English indifference to India's wrongs, and, as an illustration of this indifference, cites the fact that during the preceding year the India budget affecting the welfare of nearly three hundred millions of people was brought before Parliament on the last day of the session when only a few members were present. He asserts that "matters are far worse now than they were in the days of the old East India Company," and that "nothing short of a great famine, a terrible pestilence, or a revolt on a large scale, will induce the mass of Englishmen to devote any attention whatever to the affairs of India."

To show how, in the government of India, the interests of English office-holders outweigh the interests of the natives, I give an extract from the pamphlet already referred to:

"First, under the East India Company, and then, and far more completely, under the direct rule of the Crown of the English people, the natives have been shut out from all the principal positions of trust over five-sixths of Hindostan, and have been prevented from gaining any experience in the higher administration, or in military affairs.

"Wherever it was possible to put in an Englishman to oust a native an Englishman has been put in, and has been paid from four times to twenty times as much for his services as would have sufficed for the salary of an equally capable Hindoo or Mohammedan official. * * * At the present time, out of 39,000 officials who draw a salary of more than 1,000 rupees a year, 28,000 are Englishmen and only 11,000 natives. Moreover, the 11,000 natives receive as salaries only three million pounds a year; the 28,000 Englishmen receive fifteen million pounds a year. Out of the 960 important civil offices which really control the civil administration of India 900 are filled with Englishmen and only sixty with natives. Still worse, if possible, the natives of India have no control whatsoever in any shape or way over their own taxation, or any voice at all in the expenditure of their own revenues. Their entire government

—I speak, of course, of the 250,000,000 under our direct control —is carried on and administered by foreigners, who not only do not settle in the country, but who live lives quite remote from those of the people, and return home at about forty-five or fifty years of age with large pensions.

"As I have often said in public, India is, in fact, now governed by successive relays of English carpet-baggers, who have as little sympathy with the natives as they have any real knowledge of their habits and customs."

The Statesman's Year Book of 1897, published by Macmillan & Co., London, contains some interesting statistics in regard to India.

It seems that there are but two and a quarter millions of Christians in India—less than one per cent—after so many years of English control.

It appears, also, that in 1891 only a little more than three millions out of three hundred millions were under instruction; a little more than twelve millions were not under instruction, but able to read and write, while two hundred and forty-six millions were neither under instruction nor able to read or write. Twenty-five millions appear under the head "not returned."

The European army in India amounts to seventy-four thousand and the native army to one hundred and forty-five thousand. In the army the European officers number five thousand and the native officers twenty-seven hundred. One-fourth of the national expenditure in India goes to the support of the army. Nearly one-third of India's annual revenue is expended in Great Britain. The salary of the Governor-General is 250,-000 rupees per annum.

The Year Book above mentioned is also responsible for the statement that the act of 1893, closing the Indian mints to the free coinage of silver, was enacted by the Governor-General and Council upon the same day that it was introduced. Mr. Leech, former director of the United States mint, in an article in the Forum, declared that the closing of the mints in India on that occasion was the most momentous event in the monetary history of the present century. It will be remembered that this act was made the excuse for an extra session of our Congress and for the unconditional repeal of the Sherman law.

One can obtain some idea of the evils of irresponsible alien government when he reflects that an English Governor-General and an English Council changed the financial system of nearly three hundred millions of people by an act introduced and passed in the course of a single day.

No matter what views one may hold upon the money question, he cannot defend such a system of government without abandoning every principle revered by the founders of the republic. Senator Wolcott of Colorado, one of the President's commissioners, upon his return from Europe, made a speech in the senate in which he declared that the last Indian famine was a money famine rather than a food famine. In that speech Mr. Wolcott also asserted that the closing of the India mints reduced by five hundred millions of dollars, the value of the silver accumulated in the hands of the people. If Mr. Wolcott's statement contains the smallest fraction of truth the injury done by the East India Company during its entire existence was less than the injury done by that one act of the Governor and his Council. If the famine was, in fact. a money famine, created by an act of the Governor and his Council, then indeed is English rule as cruel and merciless in India to-day as was the rule of the East India Company's agents a century ago. English rule in India is not bad because it is English, but because no race has yet appeared sufficiently strong in character to resist the temptations which come with irresponsible power.

We may well turn from the contemplation of an imperial policy and its necessary vices to the words of Jefferson in his first inaugural message: "Sometimes it is said that man cannot be trusted with the government of himself. Can he, then, be trusted with the government of others? Or have we found angels in the form of kings to govern him? Let history answer this question."—New York Journal, Jan. 22, 1899.

---

## WHAT NEXT?

Imperialists seek to create the impression that the ratification of the treaty has terminated the controversy in regard to the future of the Philippines, but there is no ground whatever for such a conclusion. The President has not as yet outlined a policy and Congress has so far failed to make any declaration upon the subject. Several administration senators have expressly denied that ratification commits the United States to the permanent annexation of the Philippine Islands.

The treaty extinguishes Spanish sovereignty, but it does not determine our nation's course in dealing with the Filipinos. In the opinion of many (and I am among the number) the ratification of the treaty, instead of closing the door to independence, really makes easier the establishment of such a government in the Philippine Islands. The matter is now entirely within the control of Congress, and there is no legal obstacle to prevent the immediate passage of a resolution promising self-government to the Filipinos and pledging the United States to protect their government from outside interference. If we have a right to acquire land we have a right to part with it; if we have a right to secure, by purchase or conquest, a disputed title from Spain, we certainly have a right to give a quit-claim deed to the party in possession.

If the power to part with the islands is admitted, the only question remaining for discussion is whether the United States should permanently hold the Asiatic territory acquired from Spain. For two months the sentiment against imperialism has been constantly growing and there is nothing in the ratification of the treaty to make such a policy more desirable.

Until Dewey's victory no one thought us under obligation to extend our sovereignty over the Filipinos. If subsequent events have imposed such an obligation upon the United States it is worth while to inquire as to its nature and extent. Is it political in its character? Must we make subjects of the Filipinos now because we made allies of them in the war with Spain? France did not recognize any such obligation when she helped us to throw off British supremacy. Are we compelled to civilize the Filipinos by force because we interfered with Spain's efforts to accomplish the same end by the same means? Are we in duty bound to conquer and to govern, when we can find a pretext for doing so, every nation which is weaker than ours or whose civilization is below our standard? Does history justify us in believing that we can improve the condition of the Filipinos and advance them in civilization by governing them without their consent and taxing them without representation? England has tried that plan in India for a hundred and fifty years, and yet Japan has made more progress in the last thirty

55

years than India has made in the hundred and fifty. And it may be added that the idea of self-government has developed more rapidly among the Japanese during the same period than it has among the people of India.

Government is an evolution, and its administration is always susceptible of improvement. The capacity for self-government is developed by responsibility. As exercise strengthens the muscles of the athlete and as education improves the mental faculties of the student, even so participation in government instructs the citizen in the science of government and perfects him in the art of administering it.

We must not expect the Filipinos to establish and maintain as good a government as ours, and it is vain for us to expect that we would maintain there, at long range, as good a government as we have here. The government is, as it were, a composite photograph of the people, a reflection of their average virtue and intelligence.

Some defend annexation upon the ground that the business interests of the islands demand it. The business interests will probably be able to take care of themselves under an independent form of government, unless they are very different from the business interests of the United States. The so-called business men constitute a very small fraction of the total population of the islands, who will say that their pecuniary interests are superior in importance to the right of all the rest of the people to enjoy a government of their own choosing.

Some say that our duty to the foreign residents in the Philippines requires us to annex the islands. If we admit this argument we not only exalt the interests of foreigners above the interests of natives, but place a higher estimate upon the wishes of foreigners residing in Manila than upon the welfare of our own people.

The fact that the subject of imperialism is being discussed through the newspapers and magazines, as well as in Congress, is evidence that the work of education is still going on. The advocates of a colonial policy must convince the conservative element of the country, by clear and satisfactory proof, they cannot rely upon catch-words. The "Who will haul down the flag?" argument has already been discarded; "Destiny" is not as "manifest" as it was a few weeks ago, and the argument of "duty" is being analyzed. The people are face to face with a grave public problem. They have not acted upon it yet, and they will not be frightened away from the calm consideration of it by the repetition of unsupported prophesies. The battle of Manila, which brought loss to us and disaster to the Filipinos, has not rendered "forcible annexation" less repugnant to our Nation's "code of morality." If it has any effect at all it ought to emphasize the dangers attendant upon (if I may be permitted to quote from the President again) "criminal aggression." The Filipinos were guilty of inexcusable ignorance if they thought that they could prevent the ratification of the treaty by an attack upon the American lines, but no act of theirs can determine the permanent policy of the United States. Whether imperialism is desirable is too large a question to be settled by a battle. Battles are to be expected under such a policy. England had been the dominant power in India for a century, when the Sepoy mutiny took place, and she rules even now by fear rather than by love.

Force and reason rest upon different foundations and employ different forms of logic. Reason, recognizing that only that is enduring which is just, asks whether the thing proposed ought to be done; force says, I desire, I can, I will. When the desire proves to be greater than the ability to accomplish, the force argument reads (in the past tense), I desired, I tried, I failed. But even force, if accompanied by intelligence, calculates the cost. No one doubts that the United States army and navy are able to whip into subjection all the Filipinos who are not exterminated in the process, but is it worth the cost?

Militarism is only one item of the cost, but it alone will far outweigh all the advantages which are expected to flow from a colonial policy. John Morley, the English statesman, in a recent speech to his constituents, uttered a warning which may well be considered by our people. He said:

"Imperialism brings with it militarism, and must bring with it militarism. Militarism means a gigantic expenditure, daily growing. It means an increase in government of the power of aristocratic and privileged classes. Militarism means the profusion of the taxpayer's money everywhere except in the taxpayer's own home, and militarism must mean war.

"And you must be much less well read in history than I take the liberals of Scotland to be if you do not know that it is not war, that hateful demon of war, but white-winged peace that has been the nurse and guardian of freedom and justice and well-being over that great army of toilers upon whose labor, upon whose privations, upon whose hardships, after all, the greatness and the strength of empires and of states are founded and are built up."

Militarism is so necessary a companion of imperialism that the President asks for a two hundred per cent increase in the standing army, even before the people at large have passed upon the question of annexation.

Morley says that imperialism gives to the aristocracy and to the privileged classes an increased influence in government; do we need to increase their influence in our government? Surely they are potent enough already.

He calls attention to the fact that the toiler finds his hope in peaceful progress rather than in war's uncertainties. Is it strange that the laboring classes are protesting against both imperialism and militarism? Is it possible that their protest will be in vain?

Imperialism has been described as "The White Man's Burden," but, since it crushes the wealth-producer beneath an increasing weight of taxes, it might with more propriety be called The Poor Man's Load.

If the Peace Commissioners had demanded a harbor and coaling station in the Philippines and had required Spain to surrender the rest of the land to the Filipinos, as she surrendered Cuba to the Cubans, we would not now be considering how to let go of the islands. If the sum of twenty millions had been necessary to secure Spain's release, the payment of the amount by the Filipinos might have been guaranteed by the United States.

But the failure of the Peace Commissioners to secure for the Filipinos the same rights that were obtained for the Cubans, could have been easily remedied by a resolution declaring the nation's purpose to establish a stable and independent government.

It is still possible for the Senate alone, or for the Senate and House together, to adopt such a resolution.

The purpose of annexationists, so far as that purpose can be discovered, is to apply to the government of the Filipinos methods familiar to the people of Europe and Asia, but new in the United States.

This departure from traditions was not authorized by the people; whether it will be ratified by them remains to be seen. The responsibility rests first upon Congress and afterwards upon that power which makes Congresses.

Whatever may be the wish of individuals or the interests of parties, we may rest assured that the final disposition of the Philippine question will conform to the deliberate judgment of the voters; they constitute the court of last resort; from their decision there is no appeal.

What next? Investigation, discussion, action.—New York Journal, Feb. 12, 1899.

# THE PUERTO RICAN TARIFF LAW.

If the sentiment of Republican leaders is accurately reflected by the resolution reported by the Ways and Means Committee of the House, making a difference between the tariff duty in Puerto Rico and the tariff duty in the United States, the party is taking an open and bold step toward an imperial policy.

Webster, in defining an empire, says that it always comprises "variety in the nationality of, or the forms of administration in, constituent and subordinate portions."

When the Queen of Great Britain assumed dominion over India she added to her former title "Empress of India." Under the English theory of government, power descends from the throne, and the subject exercises such authority as the sovereign surrenders to him. Such a government can govern the people of England in one way, the people of Ireland in another way, the people of Canada in another way, and the people of India in still another and different way; in this country, however, power emanates from the people, and authority is conferred by the people upon those who, from time to time, hold office. The Constitution created the office of Chief Executive, granted authority to the occupant of the office, and strictly defined and limited his powers. To say that he can exercise a power not conferred by the Constitution is to say that the creature is greater than the creator.

## THE POWER OF OUR CONGRESS.

The Constitution also created a legislative body and divided it into two branches, a Senate and a House of Representatives; it conferred upon the legislative bodies the power to act upon certain questions and defined and limited the power of each body.

The Constitution, in Article 1, Section 8, provides:

"The Congress shall have power to lay and collect taxes, duties, imposts and excises, to pay debts and provide for the common defense and general welfare of the United States; but all duties, imposts and excises shall be uniform throughout the United States."

This section gives to Congress the power to collect uniform duties. Where does Congress obtain the power to collect duties which are not uniform? What power has a member of Congress more than any other citizen, except as that power is conferred by the Constitution?

When the President or Congress does anything which is unauthorized, the thing done cannot be called a law, because a law is the act of the people or of their representatives acting within the limit of authority. An unauthorized act of a public servant is personal and individual.

To say that this nation can do anything that any other nation can do must be understood with this limitation, namely, that while it deals with other nations as an equal our public servants must deal with their own people as servants deal with their masters.

In an unlimited monarchy the monarch can do anything that he has the physical power to do. In a republic an official can do only what the people authorize him to do. Constitutions are of no avail if they can be set aside by those who temporarily hold the offices created by constitutions. Whenever the American people desire to do so, they can amend the Constitution in the manner provided by the Constitution, but there is no constitutional method by which a public official can soar above the Constitution, burrow under it or go around it.

---

## OBJECTS TO PUERTO RICO TAX.

To impose upon the people of Puerto Rico such taxes as Congress may determine when the people of Puerto Rico have no representative in Congress is to assert either that taxation without representation is right, or that it is wise for us to do wrong.

The preamble of the Constitution says:

"We, the people of the United States, in order to form a more perfect union, establish justice, insure domestic tranquillity, provide for the common defence, promote the general welfare, and secure the blessings of liberty to ourselves and our posterity, do ordain and establish this Constitution for the United States of America."

It was the act of "the people of the United States," and they were acting for themselves and for posterity. It was evidently intended for a people who desired to govern themselves, not for a people desirous of governing somebody else.

If the people of the United States wish to enter upon a career of empire and possess the physical force necessary for such a career, they need not consult the Constitution at all, because force knows no law. The strongest nation has the physical right (if the word "right" can be used in such a connection) to do what it pleases, but the people of this nation have never decided to enter upon an imperial career.

When the present Congress was elec ed, in November, 1898, the treaty with Spain had not been signed, and, therefore, the question of imperialism could not have been presented to the voters.

If the Republican leaders in Congress act without authority from the Constitution, they must do so with a full recognition of the fact that the people who make constitutions and who elect public officials, will have a chance to speak before a republic is converted into an empire.

---

## DECLARES UNIFORM TAX WISE.

Uniformity in our tax laws is not only legally necessary, but it is wise. Unless the people of Puerto Rico share in the guarantees of our Constitution and in the benefits, as well as burdens, of our laws, they have no protection whatever against injustice and oppression.

Secretary Root, in his annual report, declares that the transfer of Puerto Rico from Spain to the United States has thus far brought adversity rather than prosperity to the people of the island, and says that "the highest considerations of justice and good faith demand that we should not disappoint the confident expectation of sharing in our prosperity with which the people of Puerto Rico so gladly transferred their allegiance to the United States, and that we should treat the interests of these people as our own."

He urges the removal of all custom duties between Puerto Rico and the United States. Even under this system, the people of Puerto Rico would have to pay such taxes as we imposed, but the taxes would be only such as we imposed upon ourselves and our own interests would afford some protection, although incomplete. But what is to be said of the benevolence of a colonial system which would force upon the people of Puerto Rico a condition worse than that from which we delivered them?

The President in his message to Congress said:

"Our plain duty is to abolish all customs tariffs between the United States and Puerto Rico and give her products free access to our markets."

---

## "IMPERIALISTS" SEE OUR DUTY.

It is fortunate for the American people that they have an early opportunity to measure the weakness of "the highest considerations of justice and good faith" and "our plain duty" when they come into conflict with the personal and pecuniary interests of people in this country who can make their influence felt in campaigns.

Imperialists are always telling us about our duty, as if they were able to measure it with exactness by metes and bounds, and only intent upon performing it. They prate about their unselfish love for inferior races and their determination to act as the guardians of these "children" intrusted to their care by a discriminating and considerate Providence. It is fortunate for our own people and for the new people with whom we have to deal that this mask of hypocrisy and false pretense is torn away so behind it can be seen the features of greed.

If this is to be the reward of those who "so gladly transferred their allegiance to the United States," what is to be expected by the "sullen people," who prefer the horrors of war to the blessings of peace, coupled with alien domination?

Sometimes it is difficult to determine what is one's duty in a trying position, but a "plain duty," such as the President describes, ought not to be abandoned unless it conflicts with "manifest destiny," which, in the opinion of imperialists, rises to superior duty, moral or political, no matter how plain that duty may be.

---

## SEES INJUSTICE IN EXPANSION.

The position taken by the Republican committee, however, is necessary if an imperial policy is to be pursued. The more bold advocates of imperialism regard the conquest of the Philippines as a step only toward the extension of our authority in the Orient. They are contemplating the taking of a slice of China. In fact, there is no limit to the ambition of an imperialist.

With money making as his object, he is willing to declare himself the appointed agent of the Almighty to conquer and hold in subjection any weaker people for the purpose of securing their trade. As he cannot make the laws which suit us suit them also, he is compelled to resort to diversity. He proposes such laws as will in his judgment help our trade, regardless of the effect of those laws upon the people.

If all annexed territory is given a territorial form of government with the understanding that the territorial form is merely a preparation for complete statehood, then no annexation will be tolerated, unless the people who are to come in are capable of sharing in the full destiny of our people.

In annexation two questions are to be considered: First, do the people to be annexed desire to come in, and, second, are we willing to have them come in?

Trade does not depend upon the flag. During the last quarter of a century our trade has expanded wonderfully without any extension of the nation's sovereignty. Neither is it necessary for us to extend our sovereignty in order to give assistance to those who desire to govern themselves, and set out to perfect themselves in the art of self-government.

## OUR EXAMPLE AN INSPIRATION.

Our example has already been an inspiration to millions. Because our forefathers fought for liberty others have fought for it; because our Declaration of Independence was promulgated, other declarations of independence have been promulgated; because our Constitution was established, other constitutions have been established. Not only have we set an example, but in the establishment of the Monroe doctrine we have been able to give to smaller republics the protection of this, the greatest Republic of history. We have not interfered in the government of Mexico and the South and Central American republics, and yet by the simple announcement that any attack upon their integrity would be considered an act of unfriendliness to us we have protected them from foes without.

During the last one hundred years this nation has been the most potent factor in the world's progress. As the nation's population, wealth and influence increase, its power to do good will increase, but to accomplish this end it must remain true to its principles and not descend to the level of empires and monarchies.

---

## NEW PEOPLES MUST BE RAISED.

When this nation incorporates new peoples within its limits, the new peoples must be raised to the level of our people. The line between citizen and subject is the line between republic and empire. If we accept the theory that half of our people can be free and half vassal, the vassal idea will grow until the divine right of the American people to rule distant and subject races will blossom into the doctrine that some strong man has the divine right to rule the American people, and then the people at home will become targets for the large army raised to support a policy of exploitation in other lands.

This Republic can have no higher destiny than to be a light unto the struggling and the oppressed in every land. It can win the highest glory by being a moral factor among the nations of the world, casting its influence always upon the side of those who believe in the doctrines set forth in our Declaration of Independence.

American principles are above price; American duty is not a football to be kicked first in one direction and then another by whichever financial interest happens to be strongest.

W. J. BRYAN.

New York Journal, Feb. 11, 1900.

# IMPERIALISM

### BEING THE SPEECH OF

## HON. WILLIAM JENNINGS BRYAN

In response to the committee
appointed to notify him of his
nomination to the Presidency
of the United States, Delivered
at Indianapolis, August 8, 1900

# IMPERIALISM.

Mr. Chairman and Members of the Notification Committee:

I shall, at an early day, and in a more formal manner accept the nomination which you tender, and I shall at that time discuss the various questions covered by the Democratic platform. It may not be out of place, however, to submit a few observations at this time upon the general character of the contest before us and upon the question which is declared to be of paramount importance in this campaign.

When I say that the contest of 1900 is a contest between Democracy on the one hand and plutocracy on the other I do not mean to say that all our opponents have deliberately chosen to give to organized wealth a predominating influence in the affairs of the Government, but I do assert that on the important issues of the day the Republican party is dominated by those influences which constantly tend to substitute the worship of mammon for the protection of the rights of man.

In 1859 Lincoln said that the Republican party believed in the man and the dollar, but that in case of conflict it believed in the man before the dollar. This is the proper relation which should exist between the two. Man, the handiwork of God, comes first; money, the handiwork of man, is of inferior importance. Man is the master, money the servant, but upon all important questions today Republican legislation tends to make money the master and man the servant.

The maxim of Jefferson, "equal rights to all and special privileges to none," and the doctrine of Lincoln that this should be a government "of the people, by the people and for the people," are being disregarded and the instrumentalities of government are being used to advance the interests of those who are in a position to secure favors from the Government.

## NO WAR ON THRIFT.

The Democratic party is not making war upon the honest acquisition of wealth; it has no desire to discourage industry, economy and thrift. On the contrary, it gives to every citizen the greatest possible stimulus to honest toil when it promises him protection in the enjoyment of the proceeds of his labor. Property rights are most secure when human rights are most respected. Democracy strives for civilization in which every member of society will share according to his merits.

No one has a right to expect from society more than a fair compensation for the services which he renders to society. If he secures more it is at the expense of some one else. It is no injustice to him to prevent his doing injustice to another. To him who would, either through class legislation or in the absence of necessary legislation, trespass upon the rights of another the Democratic party says, "Thou shalt not."

Against us are arrayed a comparatively small but politically and financially powerful number who really profit by Republican policies; but with them are associated a large number who, because of their attachment to their party name, are giving their support to doctrines antagonistic to the former teachings of their own party.

---

## REPUBLICAN INCONSISTENCIES.

Republicans who used to advocate bimetallism now try to convince themselves that the gold standard is good; Republicans who were formerly attached to the greenback are now seeking an excuse for giving national banks control of the nation's paper money; Republicans who used to boast that the Republican party was paying off the national debt are now looking for reasons to support a perpetual and increasing debt; Republicans who formerly abhorred a trust now beguile themselves with the delusion that there are good trusts and bad trusts, while, in their minds, the line between the two is becoming more and more obscure; Republicans who, in times past, congratulated the country upon the small expense of our standing army, are now making light of the objections which are urged against a large increase in the permanent military establishment; Republicans who gloried in our independence when the nation. was less powerful now look with favor upon a foreign alliance; Republicans who three years ago condemned "forcible annexation" as immoral and even criminal are now sure that it is both immoral and criminal to oppose forcible annexation. That partisanship has already blinded many to present dangers is certain; how large a portion of the Republican party can be drawn over to the new policies remains to be seen.

For a time Republican leaders were inclined to deny to opponents the right to criticise the Philippine policy of the administration, but upon investigation they found that both Lincoln and Clay asserted and exercised the right to criticise a President during the progress of the Mexican war.

Instead of meeting the issue boldly and submitting a clear and positive plan for dealing with the Philippine question, the Republican convention adopted a platform, the larger part of which was devoted to boasting and self-congratulation.

---

## EVASIVE REPUBLICAN POLICY.

In attempting to press economic questions upon the country to the exclusion of those which involve the very structure of our government, the Republican leaders give new evidence of their abandonment of the earlier ideals of the party and of their complete subserviency to pecuniary considerations.

But they shall not be permitted to evade the stupendous and far-reaching issue which they have deliberately brought into the arena of politics. When the president, supported by a practically unanimous vote of the House and Senate, entered upon a war with Spain for the purpose of aiding the struggling patriots of Cuba, the country, without regard to party, applauded.

Although the Democrats realized that the administration would necessarily gain a political advantage from the conduct of a war which in the very nature of the case must soon end in a complete victory, they vied with the Republicans in the support which they gave to the President. When the war was over and the Republican leaders began to suggest the propriety of a colonial policy opposition at once manifested itself.

When the President finally laid before the Senate a treaty which recognized the independence of Cuba, but provided for the

71

cession of the Philippine Islands to the United States, the menace of imperialism became so apparent that many preferred to reject the treaty and risk the ills that might follow rather than take the chance of correcting the errors of the treaty by the independent action of this country.

## WHY THE TREATY WAS RATIFIED.

I was among the number of those who believed it better to ratify the treaty and end the war, release the volunteers, remove the excuse for war expenditures and then give the Filipinos the independence which might be forced from Spain by a new treaty.

In view of the criticism which my action aroused in some quarters, I take this occasion to restate the reasons given at that time. I thought it safer to trust the American people to give independence to the Filipinos than to trust the accomplishment of that purpose to diplomacy with an unfriendly nation.

Lincoln embodied an argument in the question when he asked, "Can aliens make treaties easier than friends can make laws?" I believe that we are now in a better position to wage a successful contest against imperialism than we would have been had the treaty been rejected. With the treaty ratified a clean-cut issue is presented between a government by consent and a government by force, and imperialists must bear the responsibility for all that happens until the question is settled.

If the treaty had been rejected the opponents of imperialism would have been held responsible for any international complications which might have arisen before the ratification of another treaty. But whatever difference of opinion may have existed as to the best method of opposing a colonial policy, there never was any difference as to the great importance of the question and there is no difference now as to the course to be pursued:

## HOW WAR MIGHT HAVE BEEN AVERTED.

The title of Spain being extinguished we were at liberty to deal with the Filipinos according to American principles. The Bacon resolution, introduced a month before hostilities broke out at Manila, promised independence to the Filipinos on the same terms that it was promised to the Cubans. I supported this resolution and believe that its adoption prior to the breaking out of hostilities would have prevented bloodshed, and that its adoption at any subsequent time would have ended hostilities.

If the treaty had been rejected considerable time would have necessarily elapsed before a new treaty could have been agreed upon and ratified, and during that time the question would have been agitating the public mind. If the Bacon resolution had been adopted by the Senate and carried out by the President, either at the time of the ratification of the treaty or at any time afterwards, it would have taken the question of imperialism out of politics and left the American people free to deal with their domestic problems. But the resolution was defeated by the vote of the Republican Vice-President, and from that time to this a Republican Congress has refused to take any action whatever in the matter.

When hostilities broke out at Manila Republican speakers and Republican editors at once sought to lay the blame upon those who had delayed the ratification of the treaty, and, during the progress of the war, the same Republicans have accused the opponents of imperialism of giving encouragement to the Filipinos. This is a cowardly evasion of responsibility.

If it is right for the United States to hold the Philippine Islands permanently and imitate European empires in the government of colonies, the Republican party ought to state its position and defend it, but it must expect the subject races to protest against such a policy and to resist to the extent of their ability.

---

## THE UNITED STATES A MORAL FORCE.

The Filipinos do not need any encouragement from Americans now living. Our whole history has been an encouragement, not only to the Filipinos, but to all who are denied a voice in their own government. If the Republicans are prepared to censure all who have used language calculated to make the Filipinos hate foreign domination, let them condemn the speech of Patrick Henry. When he uttered that passionate appeal, "Give me liberty or give me death," he expressed a sentiment which still echoes in the hearts of men.

73

Let them censure Jefferson: of all the statemen of history none have used words so offensive to those who would hold their fellows in political bondage. Let them censure Washington, who declared that the colonists must choose between liberty and slavery. Or, if the statute of limitations has run against the sins of Henry and Jefferson and Washington, let them censure Lincoln, whose Gettysburg speech will be quoted in defense of popular government when the present advocates of force and conquest are forgotten.

Some one has said that a truth once spoken can never be recalled. It goes on and on, and no one can set a limit to its ever-widening influence. But if it were possible to obliterate every word written or spoken in defense of the principles set forth in the Declaration of Independence, a war of conquest would still leave its legacy of perpetual hatred, for it was God himself who placed in every human heart the love of liberty. He never made a race of people so low in the scale of civilization or intelligence that it would welcome a foreign master.

---

## EFFECT OF IMPERIAL ISSUE AT HOME.

Those who would have this nation enter upon a career of empire must consider not only the effect of imperialism on the Filipinos, but they must also calculate its effects upon our own nation. We cannot repudiate the principle of self-government in the Philippines without weakening that principle here.

Lincoln said that the safety of this nation was not in its fleets, its armies, its forts, but in the spirit which prizes liberty as the heritage of all men, in all lands, everywhere, and he warned his countrymen that they could not destroy this spirit without planting the seeds of despotism at their own doors.

Even now we are beginning to see the paralyzing influence of imperialism. Heretofore this nation has been prompt to express its sympathy with those who were fighting for civil liberty. While our sphere of activity has been limited to the Western Hemisphere, our sympathies have not been bounded by the seas. We have felt it due to ourselves and to the world, as well as to those who were struggling for the right to govern themselves, to proclaim the interest which our people have, from the date of their own independence, felt in every contest between human rights and arbitrary power.

Three-quarters of a century ago, when our nation was small, the struggles of Greece aroused our people, and Webster and Clay gave eloquent expression to the universal desire for Grecian independence. In 1896 all parties manifested a lively interest in the success of the Cubans, but now when a war is in progress in South Africa, which must result in the extension of the monarchical idea, or in the triumph of a republic, the advocates of imperialism in this country dare not say a word in behalf of the Boers.

Sympathy for the Boers does not arise from any unfriendliness towards England; the American people are not unfriendly toward the people of any nation. This sympathy is due to the fact that, as stated in our platform, we believe in the principles of self-government and reject, as did our forefathers, the claims of monarchy. If this nation surrenders its belief in the universal application of the principles set forth in the Declaration of Independence, it will lose the prestige and influence which it has enjoyed among the nations as an exponent of popular government.

---

## EXPANSION CONTRASTED WITH IMPERIALISM.

Our opponents, conscious of the weakness of their cause, seek to confuse imperialism with expansion, and have even dared to claim Jefferson as a supporter of their policy. Jefferson spoke so freely and used language with such precision that no one can be ignorant of his views. On one occasion he declared. "If there be one principle more deeply rooted than any other in the mind of every American, it is that we should have nothing to do with conquest." And again he said: "Conquest is not in our principles; it is inconsistent with our government."

The forcible annexation of territory to be governed by arbitrary power differs as much from the acquisition of territory to be built up into states as a monarchy differs from a democracy. The Democratic party does not oppose expansion when expansion enlarges the area of the Republic and incorporates land which can be settled by American citizens, or adds to our population people who are willing to become citizens and are capable of discharging their duties as such.

The acquisition of the Louisiana territory, Florida, Texas and other tracts which have been secured from time to time enlarged the Republic and the Constitution followed the flag into the new territory. It is now proposed to seize upon distant territory already more densely populated than our own country and to force upon the people a government for which there is no warrant in our Constitution or our laws.

## WHITES AND THE TROPICS.

Even the argument that this earth belongs to those who desire to cultivate it and who have the physical power to acquire it cannot be invoked to justify the appropriation of the Philippine Islands by the United States. If the islands were uninhabited American citizens would not be willing to go there and till the soil. The white race will not live so near the equator. Other nations have tried to colonize in the same latitude. The Netherlands have controlled Java for three hundred years and yet to-day there are less than sixty thousand people of European birth scattered among the twenty-five million natives.

After a century and a half of English domination in India, less than one-twentieth of one per cent of the people of India are of English birth, and it requires an army of seventy thousand British soldiers to take care of the tax collectors. Spain had asserted title to the Philippine Islands for three centuries and yet when our fleet entered Manila Bay there were less than ten thousand Spaniards residing in the Philippines.

A colonial policy means that we shall send to the Philippine Islands a few traders, a few taskmasters and a few office-holders and an army large enough to support the authority of a small fraction of the people while they rule the natives.

If we have an imperial policy we must have a great standing army as its natural and necessary complement. The spirit which will justify the forcible annexation of the Philippine Islands will justify the seizure of other islands and the domination of other people, and with wars of conquest we can expect a certain, if not rapid, growth of our military establishment.

That a large permanent increase in our regular army is intended by Republican leaders is not a matter of conjecture, but a matter of fact. In his message of December 5, 1898, the President asked for authority to increase the standing army to 100,000. In 1896 the army contained about 25,000. Within two years the President asked for four times that many, and a Republican House of Representatives complied with the request after the Spanish treaty had been signed, and when no country was at war with the United States.

## THE MENACE OF A STANDING ARMY.

If such an army is demanded when an imperial policy is contemplated, but not openly avowed, what may be expected if the people encourage the Republican party by indorsing its policy at the polls?

A large standing army is not only a pecuniary burden to the people and, if accompanied by compulsory service, a constant source of irritation, but it is ever a menace to a republican form of government.

The army is the personification of force and militarism will inevitably change the ideals of the people and turn the thoughts of our young men from the arts of peace to the science of war. The government which relies for its defense upon its citizens is more likely to be just than one which has at call a large body of professional soldiers.

A small standing army and a well-equipped and well-disciplined state militia are sufficient at ordinary times, and in an emergency the nation should in the future as in the past place its dependence upon the volunteers who come from all occupations at their country's call and return to productive labor when their services are no longer required—men who fight when the country needs fighters and work when the country needs workers.

The Republican platform assumes that the Philippine Islands will be retained under American sovereignty, and we have a right to demand of the Republican leaders a discussion of the future status of the Filipino. Is he to be a citizen or a subject? Are we to bring into the body politic eight or ten million Asiatics, so different from us in race and history that amalgamation is

77

impossible? Are they to share with us in making the laws and shaping the destiny of this nation? No Republican of prominence has been bold enough to advocate such a proposition.

---

## CITIZEN OR SUBJECT?

The McEnery resolution, adopted by the Senate immediately after the ratification of the treaty, expressly negatives this idea. The Democratic platform describes the situation when it says that the Filipinos cannot be citizens without endangering our civilization. Who will dispute it? And what is the alternative? If the Filipino is not to be a citizen, shall we make him a subject? On that question the Democratic platform speaks with equal emphasis. It declares that the Filipino cannot be a subject without endangering our form of government. A Republic can have no subjects. A subject is possible only in a government resting upon force; he is unknown in a government deriving its just powers from the consent of the governed.

The Republican platform says that "the largest measure of self-government consistent with their welfare and our duties shall be secured to them (the Filipinos) by law." This is a strange doctrine for a government which owes its very existence to the men who offered their lives as a protest against government without consent and taxation without representation.

In what respect does the position of the Republican party differ from the position taken by the English government in 1776? Did not the English government promise a good government to the colonists? What king ever promised a bad government to his people? Did not the English government promise that the colonists should have the largest measure of self-government consistent with their welfare and English duties? Did not the Spanish government promise to give to the Cubans the largest measure of self-government consistent with their welfare and Spanish duties? The whole difference between a monarchy and a Republic may be summed up in one sentence. In a monarchy the king gives to the people what he believes to be a good government; in a Republic the people secure for themselves what they believe to be a good government.

## REPUBLICANS IMITATE GEORGE III.

The Republican party has accepted the European idea and planted itself upon the ground taken by George III., and by every ruler who distrusts the capacity of the people for self-government or denies them a voice in their own affairs.

The Republican platform promises that some measure of self-government is to be given the Filipinos by law; but even this pledge is not fulfilled. Nearly sixteen months elapsed after the ratification of the treaty before the adjournment of Congress last June and yet no law was passed dealing with the Philippine situation. The will of the President has been the only law in the Philippine Islands wherever the American authority extends.

Why does the Republican party hesitate to legislate upon the Philippine question? Because a law would disclose the radical departure from history and precedent contemplated by those who control the Republican party. The storm of protest which greeted the Porto Rican bill was an indication of what may be expected when the American people are brought face to face with legislation upon this subject.

If the Porto Ricans, who welcomed annexation, are to be denied the guarantees of our Constitution, what is to be the lot of the Filipinos, who resisted our authority? If secret influences could compel a disregard of our plain duty toward friendly people, living near our shores, what treatment will those same influences provide for unfriendly people 7,000 miles away? If, in this country where the people have a right to vote, Republican leaders dare not take the side of the people against the great monopolies which have grown up within the last few years, how can they be trusted to protect the Filipinos from the corporations which are waiting to exploit the islands?

---

## CUBA, PORTO RICO AND THE PHILIPPINES.

Is the sunlight of full citizenship to be enjoyed by the people of the United States, and the twilight of semi-citizenship endured by the people of Porto Rico, while the thick darkness of perpetual vassalage covers the Philippines? The Porto Rico tariff law asserts the doctrine that the operation of the Constitution is confined to the forty-five States.

The Democratic party disputes this doctrine and denounces it as repugnant to both the letter and spirit of our organic law. There is no place in our system of government for the deposit of arbitrary and irresponsible power. That the leaders of a great party should claim for any President or Congress the right to treat millions of people as mere "possessions" and deal with them unrestrained by the Constitution or the bill of rights shows how far we have already departed from the ancient landmarks and indicates what may be expected if this nation deliberately enters upon a career of empire.

The territorial form of government is temporary and preparatory, and the chief security a citizen of a territory has is found in the fact that he enjoys the same constitutional guarantees and is subject to the same general laws as the citizen of a state. Take away this security and his rights will be violated and his interests sacrificed at the demand of those who have political influence. This is the evil of the colonial system, no matter by what nation it is applied.

---

## THE FLAW IN OUR TITLE.

What is our title to the Philippine Islands? Do we hold them by treaty or by conquest? Did we buy them or did we take them? Did we purchase the people? If not, how did we secure title to them? Were they thrown in with the land? Will the Republicans say that inanimate earth has value but that when that earth is molded by the divine hand and stamped with the likeness of the Creator it becomes a fixture and passes with the soil? If governments derive their just powers from the consent of the governed, it is impossible to secure title to people, either by force or by purchase.

We could extinguish Spain's title by treaty, but if we hold title we must hold it by some method consistent with our ideas of government. When we made allies of the Filipinos and armed them to fight against Spain, we disputed Spain's title. If we buy Spain's title we are not innocent purchasers.

There can be no doubt that we accepted and utilized the services of the Filipinos, and that when we did so we had full knowledge that they were fighting for their own independence, and I submit that history furnishes no example of turpitude baser than ours if we now substitute our yoke for the Spanish yoke.

80

Let us consider briefly the reasons which have been given in support of an imperialistic policy. Some say that it is our duty to hold the Philippine Islands. But duty is not an argument; it is a conclusion. To ascertain what our duty is, in any emergency, we must apply well settled and generally accepted principles. It is our duty to avoid stealing, no matter whether the thing to be stolen is of great or little value. It is our duty to avoid killing a human being, no matter where the human being lives or to what race or class he belongs.

## THE ARGUMENT OF "DUTY."

Every one recognizes the obligation imposed upon individuals to observe both the human and the moral law, but as some deny the application of those laws to nations, it may not be out of place to quote the opinions of others. Jefferson, than whom there is no higher political authority, said:

"I know of but one code of morality for men, whether acting singly or collectively."

Franklin, whose learning, wisdom and virtue are a part of the priceless legacy bequeathed to us from the revolutionary days, expressed the same idea in even stronger language when he said:

"Justice is strictly due between neighbor nations as between neighbor citizens. A highwayman is as much a robber when he plunders in a gang as when single; and the nation that makes an unjust war is only a great gang."

Many may dare to do in crowds what they would not dare to do as individuals, but the moral character of an act is not determined by the number of those who join it. Force can defend a right, but force has never yet created a right. If it was true, as declared in the resolutions of intervention, that the Cubans "are and of right ought to be free and independent" (language taken from the Declaration of Independence), it is equally true that the Filipinos "are and of right ought to be free and independent."

## THE RIGHT TO FREEDOM.

The right of the Cubans to freedom was not based upon their proximity to the United States, nor upon the language which they spoke, nor yet upon the race or races to which they belonged. Congress by a practically unanimous vote declared that the principles enunciated at Philadelphia in 1776 were still alive and applicable to the Cubans. Who will draw a line between the natural rights of the Cubans and the Filipinos? Who will say that the former has a right to liberty and that the latter has no rights which we are bound to respect? And, if the Filipinos "are and of right ought to be free and independent," what right have we to force our government upon them without their consent? Before our duty can be ascertained their rights must be determined, and when their rights are once determined it is as much our duty to respect those rights as it was the duty of Spain to respect the rights of the people of Cuba or the duty of England to respect the rights of the American colonists. Rights never conflict; duties never clash. Can it be our duty to usurp political rights which belong to others? Can it be our duty to kill those who, following the example of our forefathers, love liberty well enough to fight for it?

Some poet has described the terror which overcame a soldier who in the midst of the battle discovered that he had slain his brother. It is written "All ye are brethren." Let us hope for the coming of the day when human life—which when once destroyed cannot be restored—will be so sacred that it will never be taken except when necessary to punish a crime already committed, or to prevent a crime about to be committed.

It is said that we have assumed before the world obligations which make it necessary for us to permanently maintain a government in the Philippine Islands. I reply first, that the highest obligation of this nation is to be true to itself. No obligation to any particular nations, or to all the nations combined, can require the abandonment of our theory of government, and the substitution of doctrines against which our whole national life has been a protest. And, second, that our obligation to the Filipinos, who inhabit the islands, is greater than any obligation which we can owe to foreigners who have a temporary residence in the Philippines or desire to trade there.

It is argued by some that the Filipinos are incapable of self-government and that, therefore, we owe it to the world to take control of them. Admiral Dewey, in an official report to the Navy Department, declared the Filipinos more capable of self-government than the Cubans, and said that he based his opinion upon a knowledge of both races. But I will not rest the case upon the relative advancement of the Filipinos. Henry Clay, in defending the right of the people of South America to self-government, said:

## "THE ARGUMENT OF THRONES."

"It is the doctrine of thrones that man is too ignorant to govern himself. Their partisans assert his incapacity in reference to all nations; if they cannot command universal assent to the proposition, it is then demanded to particular nations; and our pride and our presumption too often make converts of us. I contend that it is to arraign the disposition of Providence himself to suppose that he has created beings incapable of governing themselves, and to be trampled on by kings. Self-government is the natural government of man."

Clay was right. There are degrees of proficiency in the art of self-government, but it is a reflection upon the Creator to say that he denied to any people the capacity of self-government. Once admit that some people are capable of self-government and that others are not and that the capable people have a right to seize upon and govern the incapable, and you make force—brute force—the only foundation of government and invite the reign of a despot. I am not willing to believe that an all-wise and an all-loving God created the Filipinos and then left them thousands of years helpless until the islands attracted the attention of European nations.

Republicans ask, "Shall we haul down the flag that floats over our dead in the Philippines?" The same question might have been asked when the American flag floated over Chapultepec and waved over the dead who fell there; but the tourist who visits the City of Mexico finds there a national cemetery owned by the United States and cared for by an American citizen.

Our flag still floats over our dead, but when the treaty with Mexico was signed American authority withdrew to the Rio Grande, and I venture the opinion that during the last fifty years the people of Mexico have made more progress under the stimulus of independence and self-government than they would have made under a carpet-bag government held in place by bayonets. The United States and Mexico, friendly republics, are each stronger and happier than they would have been had the

83

former been cursed and the latter crushed by an imperialistic policy disguised as "benevolent assimilation."

---

## MIGHT AND RIGHT.

"Can we not govern colonies?" we are asked. The question is not what we can do, but what we ought to do. This nation can do whatever it desires to do, but it must accept responsibility for what it does. If the Constitution stands in the way, the people can amend the Constitution. I repeat, the nation can do whatever it desires to do, but it cannot avoid the natural and legitimate results of its own conduct.

The young man upon reaching his majority can do what he pleases. He can disregard the teachings of his parents; he can trample upon all that he has been taught to consider sacred: he can disobey the laws of the State, the laws of society and the laws of God. He can stamp failure upon his life and make his very existence a curse to his fellow men, and he can bring his father and mother in sorrow to the grave; but he cannot annul the sentence, "The wages of sin is death."

And so with the nation. It is of age and it can do what it pleases; it can spurn the traditions of the past; it can repudiate the principles upon which the nation rests; it can employ force instead of reason; it can substitute might for right; it can conquor weaker people; it can exploit their lands, appropriate their property and kill their people; but it cannot repeal the moral law or escape the punishment decreed for the violation of human rights.

"Would we tread in the paths of tyrany,
    Nor reckon the tyrant's cost?
Who taketh another's liberty
    His freedom is also lost.
Would we win as the strong have ever won,
    Make ready to pay the debt,
For the God who reigned over Babylon
    Is the God who is reigning yet.

---

## WE DARE NOT EDUCATE THE FILIPINOS.

Some argue that American rule in the Philippine Islands will result in the better education of the Filipinos. Be not deceived. If we expect to maintain a colonial policy, we shall not find it to our advantage to educate the people. The educated

84

Filipinos are now in revolt against us, and the most ignorant ones have made the least resistance to our domination. If we are to govern them without their consent and give them no voice in determining the taxes which they must pay, we dare not educate them, lest they learn to read the Declaration of Independence and Constitution of the United States and mock us for our inconsistency.

The principal arguments, however, advanced by those who enter upon a defense of imperialism are:

First—That we must improve the present opportunity to become a world power and enter into international politics.

Second—That our commercial interests in the Philippine Islands and in the Orient make it necessary for us to hold the islands permanently.

Third—That the spread of the Christian religion will be facilitated by a colonial policy.

Fourth—That there is no honorable retreat from the position which the nation has taken.

The first argument is addressed to the nation's pride and the second to the nation's pocket-book. The third is intended for the church member and the fourth for the partisan.

---

OUR PLACE IN WORLD POLITICS.

It is sufficient answer to the first argument to say that for more than a century this nation has been a world power. For ten decades it has been the most potent· influence in the world. Not only has it been a world power, but it has done more to affect the politics of the human race than all the other nations of the world combined. Because our Declaration of Independence was promulgated others have been promulgated. Because the patriots of 1776 fought for liberty others have fought for it. Because our Constitution was adopted other constitutions have been adopted.

The growth of the principle of self-government, planted on American soil, has been the overshadowing political fact of the nineteenth century. It has made this nation conspicuous among the nations and given it a place in history such as no other nation has ever enjoyed. Nothing has been able to check the onward march of this idea. I am not willing that this nation shall cast aside the ominpotent weapon of truth to seize again the weapons of physical warfare. I would not exchange the glory of this Republic for the glory of all the empires that have risen and fallen since time began.

The permanent chairman of the last Republican National Convention presented the pecuniary argument in all its baldness when he said:

"We make no hypocritical pretense of being interested in the Philippines solely on account of others. While we regard the welfare of those people as a sacred trust, we regard the welfare of the American people first. We see our duty to ourselves as well as to others. We believe in trade expansion. By every legitimate means within the province of government and constitution we mean to stimulate the expansion of our trade and open new markets."

This is the commercial argument. It is based upon the theory that war can be rightly waged for pecuniary advantage, and that it is profitable to purchase trade by force and violence. Franklin denied both of these propositions. When Lord Howe asserted that the acts of Parliament which brought on the Revolution were necessary to prevent American trade from passing into foreign channels, Franklin replied:

---

FRANKLIN ON BARTERING BLOOD FOR TRADE.

"To me it seems that neither the obtaining nor retaining of any trade, howsoever valuable, is an object for which men may justly spill each other's blood; that the true and sure means of extending and securing commerce are the goodness and cheapness of commodities, and that the profits of no trade can ever be equal to the expense of compelling it and holding it by fleets and armies. I consider this war against us, therefore, as both unjust and unwise."

I place the philosophy of Franklin against the sordid doctrine of those who would put a price upon the head of an American soldier and justify a war of conquest upon the ground that it will pay. The Democratic party is in favor of the expansion of trade. It would extend our trade by every legitimate and peaceful means; but it is not willing to make merchandise of human blood.

86

But a war of conquest is as unwise as it is unrighteous. A harbor and coaling station in the Philippines would answer every trade and military necessity and such a concession could have been secured at any time without difficulty.

It is not necessary to own people in order to trade with them. We carry on trade to-day with every part of the world, and our commerce has expanded more rapidly than the commerce of any European empire. We do not own Japan or China, but we trade with their people. We have not absorbed the republics of Central and South America, but we trade with them. It has not been necessary to have any political connection with Canada or the nations of Europe in order to trade with them. Trade cannot be permanently profitable unless it is voluntary.

When trade is secured by force, the cost of securing it and retaining it must be taken out of the profits, and the profits are never large enough to cover the expense. Such a system would never be defended but for the fact that the expense is borne by all the people, while the profits are enjoyed by a few.

Imperialism would be profitable to the army contractors; it would be profitable to the ship owners, who would carry live soldiers to the Philippines and bring dead soldiers back; it would be profitable to those who would seize upon the franchises, and it would be profitable to the officials whose salaries would be fixed here and paid over there; but to the farmer, to the laboring man and to the vast majority of those engaged in other occupations it would bring expenditure without return and risk without reward.

Farmers and laboring men have, as a rule, small incomes and under systems which place the tax upon consumption pay much more than their fair share of the expenses of government. Thus the very people who receive least benefit from imperialism will be injured most by the military burdens which accompany it.

In addition to the evils which he and the former share in common, the laboring man will be the first to suffer if oriental subjects seek work in the United States; the first to suffer if American capital leaves our shores to employ oriental labor in the Philippines to supply the trade of China and Japan, the first to suffer from the violence which the military spirit arouses and the first to suffer when the methods of imperialism are applied to our own government.

87

It is not strange, therefore, that the labor organizations have been quick to note the approach of these dangers and prompt to protest against both militarism and imperialism.

The pecuniary argument, though more effective with certain classes, is not likely to be used so often or presented with so much enthusiasm as the religious argument. If what has been termed the "gunpowder gospel" were urged against the Filipinos only it would be a sufficient answer to say that a majority of the Filipinos are now members of one branch of the Christian church; but the principle involved is one of much wider application and challenges serious consideration.

## THE RELIGIOUS ARGUMENT.

The religious argument varies in positiveness from a passive belief that Providence delivered the Filipinos into our hands for their good and our glory to the exultation of the minister who said that we ought to "thrash the natives (Filipinos) until they understand who we are," and that "every bullet sent, every cannon shot and every flag waved means righteousness."

We cannot approve of this doctrine in one place unless we are willing to apply it everywhere. If there is poison in the blood of the hand it will ultimately reach the heart. It is equally true that forcible Christianity, if planted under the American flag in the far-away Orient, will sooner or later be transplanted upon American soil.

If true Christianity consists in carrying out in our daily lives the teachings of Christ, who will say that we are commanded to civilize with dynamite and proselyte with the sword? He who would declare the divine will must prove his authority either by Holy Writ or by evidence of a special dispensation.

Imperialism finds no warrant in the bible. The command "Go ye into all the world and preach the gospel to every creature" has no Gatling gun attachment. When Jesus visited a village of Samaria and the people refused to receive him, some of the disciples suggested that fire should be called down from heaven to avenge the insult; but the Master rebuked them and said: "Ye know not what manner of spirit ye are of; for the Son of Man is not come to destroy men's lives, but to save them." Suppose he had said: "We will thrash them until they understand who we are," how different would have been the history of Christianity! Compare, if you will, the swaggering, bullying, brutal doctrine of imperialism with the golden rule and the commandment "Thou shalt love thy neighbor as thyself."

Love, not force, was the weapon of the Nazarene; sacrifice for others, not the exploitation of them, was His method of reaching the human heart. A missionary recently told me that the Stars and Stripes once saved his life because his assailant recognized our flag as a flag that had no blood upon it.

Let it be known that our missionaries are seeking souls instead of sovereignty; let it be known that instead of being the advance guard of conquering armies, they are going forth to help and uplift, having their loins girt about with truth and their feet shod with the preparation of the gospel of peace, wearing the breastplate of righteousness and carrying the sword of the spirit; let it be known that they are citizens of a nation which respects the rights of the citizens of other nations as carefully as it protects the rights of its own citizens, and the welcome given to our missionaries will be more cordial than the welcome extended to the missionaries of any other nation.

The argument made by some that it was unfortunate for the nation that it had anything to do with the Philippine Islands, but that the naval victory at Manila made the permanent acquisition of those islands necessary, is also unsound. We won a naval victory at Santiago, but that did not compel us to hold Cuba.

The shedding of American blood in thePhilippine Islands does not make it imperative that we should retain possession forever; American blood was shed at San Juan Hill and El Caney, and yet the President has promised the Cubans independence. The fact that the American flag floats over Manila does not compel us to exercise perpetual sovereignty over the islands : the American flag waves over Havana to-day, but the President has promised to haul it down when the flag of the Cuban Republic is ready to rise in its place. Better a thousand times that our flag in the Orient give way to a flag representing the idea of self-government than that the flag of this Republic should become the flag of an empire.

# THE SOLUTION OF THE PROBLEM.

There is an easy, honest, honorable solution of the Philippine question. It is set forth in the Democratic platform and it is submitted with confidence to the American people. This plan I unreservedly indorse. If elected, I will convene congress in extraordinary session as soon as inaugurated and recommend an immediate declaration of the nation's purpose, first, to establish a stable form of government in the Philippine Islands, just as we are now establishing a stable form of government in Cuba; second, to give independence to the Cubans; third, to protect the Filipinos from outside interference while they work out their destiny, just as we have protected the republics of Central and South America, and are, by the Monroe doctrine, pledged to protect Cuba.

A European protectorate often results in the plundering of the ward by the guardian. An American protectorate gives to the nation protected the advantage of our strength, without making it the victim of our greed. For three-quarters of a century the Monroe doctrine has been a shield to neighboring republics and yet it has imposed no pecuniary burden upon us. After the Filipinos had aided us in the war against Spain, we could not honorably turn them over to their former masters; we could not leave them to be the victims of the ambitious designs of European nations, and since we do not desire to make them a part of us or to hold them as subjects, we propose the only alternative, namely, to give them independence and guard them against molestation from without.

When our opponents are unable to defend their position by argument they fall back upon the assertion that it is destiny, and insist that we must submit to it, no matter how much it violates our moral precepts and our principles of government. This is a complacent philosophy. It obliterates the distinction between right and wrong and makes individuals and nations the helpless victims of circumstance.

---

## THE PLEA OF "DESTINY."

Destiny is the subterfuge of the invertebrate, who, lacking the courage to oppose error, seeks some plausible excuse for supporting it. Washington said that the destiny of the republican form of government was deeply, if not finally, staked on the experiment entrusted to the American people. How different Washington's definition of destiny from the Republican definition!

The Republicans say that this nation is in the hands of destiny; Washington believed that not only the destiny of our own nation but the destiny of the republican form of government throughout the world was intrusted to American hands. Immeasureable responsibility! The destiny of this republic is in the hands of its own people, and upon the success of the experiment here rests the hope of humanity. No exterior force can disturb this Republic, and no foreign influence should be permitted to change its course. What the future has in store for this nation no one has authority to declare, but each individual has his own idea of the nation's mission, and he owes it to his country as well as to himself to contribute as best he may to the fulfillment of that mission.

Mr. Chairman and Gentlemen of the Committee: I can never fully discharge the debt of gratitude which I owe to my countrymen for the honors which they have so generously bestowed upon me; but, sirs, whether it be my lot to occupy the high office for which the convention has named me, or to spend the remainder of my days in private life, it shall be my constant ambition and my controlling purpose to aid in realizing the high ideals of those whose wisdom and courage and sacrifices brought this Republic into existence.

I can conceive of a national destiny surpassing the glories of the present and the past—a destiny which meets the responsibilities of today and measures up to the possibilities of the future. Behold a republic, resting securely upon the foundation stones quarried by revolutionary patriots from the mountain of eternal truth—a republic applying in practice and proclaiming to the world the self-evident proposition that all men are created equal; that they are endowed with inalienable rights; that governments are instituted among men to secure these rights, and that governments derive their just powers from the consent of the governed. Behold a republic in which civil and religious liberty stimulate all to earnest endeavor and in which the law restrains every hand uplifted for a neighbor's injury— a republic in which every citizen is a sovereign, but in which no one cares to wear a crown. Behold a republic standing erect while empires all around are bowed beneath the weight of their own armaments—a republic whose flag is loved while other flags are only feared. Behold a republic increasing in population, in wealth, in strength, and in influence, solving the problems of civilization and hastening the coming of an universal brotherhood—a republic which shakes thrones and dissolves aristocracies by its silent example and gives light and inspiration to those who sit in darkness. Behold a republic gradually but surely becoming a supreme moral factor in the world's progress and the accepted arbiter of the world's disputes—a republic whose history, like the path of the just, "is as the shining light that shineth more and more unto the perfect day."